INTRODUCTION TO SMALL AREA ESTIMATION TECHNIQUES

A Practical Guide for National Statistics Offices

MAY 2020

ADB

ASIAN DEVELOPMENT BANK

CONTENTS

TABLES, FIGURES, AND BOXES

TABLES

FIGURES

BOXES

FOREWORD

From 2000 to 2015, the Millennium Development Goals (MDGs) influenced global development strategies by setting concrete, time-specific, and measurable targets.

By 2015, the MDGs had achieved substantial progress in poverty reduction and other areas of socio-economic development. In education and health, for instance, the number of out-of-school children of primary school age and the mortality rate for children aged under 5 years had decreased since 1990. Although data for the MDGs generated intercountry comparisons across various social and economic metrics, the absence of granular data meant that they fell short in showing how disparities within each country differed over time. This offered scarce empirical evidence on which sector of a country's population advanced or trailed behind in relation to the MDGs, and provided insufficient data to inform the development of appropriate programs for vulnerable segments of the population. To address this concern, the 2030 Sustainable Development Agenda pledged that "no one will be left behind," and called for more granular data by measuring specific Sustainable Development Goal (SDG) indicators for various clusters of the population (i.e., based on income level, ethnicity, geographic area and other groups relevant to the national context).

Many techniques can generate granular-level SDG data, and each strategy requires different levels of accuracy and data specifications. For survey-based estimates, data granularity implies that the survey sufficiently represents samples from each subgroup of the population. However, most national statistics offices (NSOs) in developing nations are resource-constrained and may not be able to conduct large enough surveys to generate reliable estimates for various subgroups of the population. In such cases, small area estimation methodologies can provide more reliable granular level estimates by "borrowing strength" from other data collection vehicles with more comprehensive coverage, thus artificially increasing the survey sample size.

This document serves as a step-by-step guide on how to implement basic small area estimation methods and highlights important considerations when executing each technique. Brief discussions of underlying theories and statistical principles are complemented with practical examples to reinforce the readers' learning process. Due to increasing popularity of usage of R among development statisticians and researchers, software implementation using R is also demonstrated throughout this guide.

This guide is intended for staff of NSOs who are compiling granular statistics needed for SDG data monitoring. The users of this guide are expected to have knowledge of basic concepts of regression modeling. We hope this guide will enrich the portfolio of analytical tools available to NSOs and contribute to increased availability of detailed frameworks for the disaggregation of SDG data.

Yasuyuki Sawada
Chief Economist and Director General
Economic Research and Regional Cooperation Department
Asian Development Bank

ACKNOWLEDGMENTS

Preparation of *Introduction to Small Area Estimation Techniques: A Practical Guide for National Statistics Offices* was undertaken by the Statistics and Data Innovation Unit of the Economic Research and Regional Cooperation Department at the Asian Development Bank (ADB) and supported by Knowledge and Support Technical Assistance (KSTA) 9356: Data for Development. Arturo Martinez, Jr. led the publication of this guide under the overall direction of Kaushal Joshi and with technical support from Joseph Bulan, Criselda De Dios, and Iva Sebastian.

ADB acknowledges the valuable contribution of Zita Albacea, who prepared the first draft of this guide, and project team members Mildred Addawe, Joseph Bulan, Ron Lester Durante, Jan Arvin Lapuz, Marymell Martillan, Arturo Martinez Jr., and Katrina Miradora, who finalized the guide. We also thank Jose Ramon Albert, Erniel Barrios and Joseph Ryan Lansangan for technical advice, detailed reviews, and relevant documents that served as references in preparing this guide.

We gratefully acknowledge substantial input from Oarawan Sutthangkul, Budsara Sangaroon, Saowaluck Inbumrung, Sanonoi Buracharoen, Thitiwat Kaew-Amdee, Bunpot Teemuangsong, and Saratrai Watcharaporn in the National Statistical Office of Thailand, and Philippine Statistics Authority (PSA) management and staff, Claire Dennis Mapa, Candido Astrologo, Jr., Wilma Guillen, Minerva Eloisa Esquivias, Bernadette Balamban, Mechelle Viernes, Anna Jean Pascasio and Driesch Cortel for improving the guide's structure and ensuring its usefulness for NSO staff. We also thank SAE training workshop participants for providing valuable comments and feedback.

We are also grateful to Rhommel Rico for conceptualizing the cover design, Karen Williams for copyediting, and Judy Yñiguez for typesetting. We acknowledge the publishing team of ADB's Department of Communications for performing overall compliance checks, and the Logistics Management Unit of the Office of Administrative Services for facilitating timely printing of the guide. We also thank Ma. Roselia Babalo, Rose Anne Dumayas, Oth Marulou Gagni, Aileen Gatson, and Charmaine Payuyo for administrative support.

Finally, we acknowledge the national statistical systems for continuously providing more granular data that facilitate targeted policymaking.

Elaine Tan
Advisor, Office of the Chief Economist and Director General,
and Head, Statistics and Data Innovation Unit,
Economic Research and Regional Cooperation Department
Asian Development Bank

ABBREVIATIONS

ADB	Asian Development Bank
BARE	broad area ratio estimator
CPH	Census of Population and Housing
CRAN	Comprehensive R Archive Network
EBLUP	empirical best linear unbiased prediction
ELL	Elbers, Lanjouw and Lanjouw
FIES	Family Income and Expenditure Survey
HIES	Household Income and Expenditure Survey
MDG	Millennium Development Goal
MSE	mean square error
NESDB	National Economic and Social Development Board
NSO	National Statistics Office
OLS	ordinary least squares
PSA	Philippine Statistics Authority
PSU	primary sampling unit
SAE	small area estimation
SDG	Sustainable Development Goal
UNESCAP	United Nations Economic and Social Commission for Asia and the Pacific
UNICEF	United Nations Children's Fund
VIF	variance inflation factor
WHO	World Health Organization
WLS	weighted least squares

CHAPTER

I | INTRODUCTION

Statistics provide important inputs for evidence-based policymaking because they comprise an integral part of designing, monitoring, and evaluating development issues surrounding social, economic, and environmental priorities. For instance, statistics on household income and/or expenditures, number of full meals per day, access to basic services, educational attainment of household members, and number of people working are commonly collected when designing poverty alleviation programs. After implementation of a poverty alleviation program, the same set of statistics could be used to evaluate the program's effectiveness.

While statistics are important ingredients of policymaking at the national level, the Millennium Development Goals (MDGs) (2000–2015) further highlighted the important role of statistics and data in realizing international development priorities. More specifically, data used to monitor MDG indicators helped identify countries that most needed galvanized development efforts and targeted interventions. Since then, both national statistical systems and the international statistical community have redoubled their efforts to use data to monitor development targets and ensure high-quality, accessible, timely, and reliable policy inputs.

Since 2015, the Sustainable Development Goals (SDGs) have provided a global development framework for expanding the progress achieved through the MDGs by addressing the social, economic, and environmental aspects of sustainable development. To ensure that this process leaves no one behind, the global indicator framework of the SDGs recommends disaggregating data according to income, sex, age, race, ethnicity, migration status, disability, geographic location, and other relevant dimensions. This recommendation also calls for enhanced granularity of statistics.

More disaggregated and granular statistics can help facilitate more efficient policy- or intervention-targeting because they focus beyond broad trends and averages toward identifying specific subgroups of the population that are not benefiting from specific development targets. However, the need for disaggregation imposes several challenges on data collection. Obviously, disaggregation requires more information to adequately represent population subgroups in the underlying calculations.

In the context of statistical indicators collected through sample surveys, disaggregation could require larger sampling. However, not all (official) statistical data collection agencies can sustain the additional administrative, financial, and technical resources that accompany larger sample sizes. Hence, national statistics offices (NSOs) should explore other cost-effective strategies to enhance granularity of statistics. A more cost-effective strategy combines multiple data sources through small area estimation (SAE). The principle behind SAE is simple. If a sample survey cannot provide an adequately precise and reliable granular or disaggregated estimate, SAE combines the survey data with other types of auxiliary data (e.g., administrative data or census data) that have wider coverage to enhance the survey estimator.

This guide provides a gentle introduction to basic SAE techniques and describes the implementation of these techniques using R software. First, it provides a rationale for conducting SAE in the context of meeting the disaggregated data requirements of the SDGs. Second, it walks readers through the basics of data management and analysis using R. Third, it presents various SAE techniques, from simple calibration methods to progressively more sophisticated modeling procedures. The discussion of each SAE technique includes several examples to demonstrate step-by-step implementation of the underlying procedure. Themes of calculation examples are drawn mainly from commonly collected household surveys (e.g., the Family Income and Expenditure Survey, the Labor Force Survey, and the Demographic and Health Survey). Software implementation using R is provided throughout the discussion.

This guide specifically targets the technical staff of NSOs, other data collection agencies that compile official statistics and SDG indicators, development practitioners, students, and researchers with some background in statistical data analysis and who are interested in granularity of statistics. For better appreciation of the technical chapters of this guide, we encourage readers with limited background in the basics of statistical models to read the Appendixes, particularly the discussion on model building.

1.1 What is Small Area Estimation and Why Do We Need It?

The first photo shows the view from a tower in Shanghai, People's Republic of China, in 2015. With over 195 billion pixels, this photograph is ultra-high resolution. At this writing, the image holds the record as the photo with the most number of pixels in Asia.

Ultra-high resolution panoramic view of Shanghai. This ultra-high resolution photograph of a view from a tower in Shanghai, People's Republic of China, in 2015 contains over 195 billion pixels (photo by Shanghai Bigpixel Technology Co., Ltd. http://www.bigpixel.cn/t/5834170785f26b37002af46d).

Indeed, this bird's-eye view of Shanghai paints a landscape of a dynamic and progressive metropolis. Zooming in on any part of the image would still provide a clear perspective. Although a lower-resolution photo could still show a clear view of the city, zooming in on a specific area could increase the overall pixilation.

Taken together, the three photos show a compelling allegory for how data collection systems that produce statistics, which serve as inputs for policymaking, could be designed versus how they are currently

Ultra-high resolution view of particular areas in Shanghai. (Photos by Shanghai Bigpixel Technology Co., Ltd.)

Low resolution view of areas in Shanghai. For low resolution photographs, zooming in on a specific area could result in overall pixilation (photos by Shanghai Bigpixel Technology Co., Ltd.), after blurring by authors.

designed. Today, many data collection systems are drawn to provide snapshots, or "big picture," estimates. For instance, survey sample sizes are typically calculated such that estimates of the parameter of interest are reliable enough nationally, regionally, or at a certain highly aggregated level. On the other hand, a census may not have the "small sample size" problem, but may still have a limited range of information. Just as capturing a high-resolution image of Shanghai comes with a cost, increasing the sample size of a survey or range of topics in a census certainly generates the need for additional financial, technical, and administrative resources. In particular, collecting more data is expected to commensurately increase the number of enumerators/interviewers, field supervisors, and even data processors, along with more data collection instruments, equipment, and gadgets. Additionally, the data collection period may be longer. Frequently, however, national statistical systems have limited resources to absorb the additional cost.

Nevertheless, we cannot underestimate the importance of rich, granular data. Availability of granular or disaggregated data enhances the efficiency of the decision-making process because they can be used as the basis in formulating policies, identifying appropriate population groups for policy targets, and monitoring the progress of an already implemented program.

Therefore, we must reconcile the need for granular data to facilitate evidence-based policymaking with the need to ensure that the cost of data collection is sustainable.

SAE provides an analytical framework for improving the level of granularity without necessarily collecting additional data in the field. This methodology integrates multiple data sources and capitalizes on the strengths of each source. Compared to a census, a survey has typically a wider range of information.

In fact, NSOs use surveys to gather detailed information on household income, expenditures, working conditions, and health, among other things. However, survey estimates are subject to margin of error because a survey does not get information from every unit of its target population. On the other hand, a census may completely enumerate all units of its target population but lack sufficient detail about the characteristic of interest. In SAE, a survey borrows strength from the wide coverage of a census, yielding estimates that remain reliable even when disaggregated at levels, or "small areas", for which the survey was not originally designed to provide reliable estimates.

Although small area generally refers to a more granular geographic location (e.g., a county, municipality, or census division), it may also pertain to a "small domain" (e.g., an age-sex-ethnic group of persons living in a large geographical location) (Gosh and Rao 1994). Typically, the sample size of a small area is much smaller than the sample size at the survey domain level. For instance, suppose a survey was designed to provide reliable estimates at the regional level. Hence, the region serves as the survey's domain and sample size is calculated for each region in the target population. If a region contains multiple provinces, then a province can be considered as a small area because the survey may not have enough sample size to yield reliable estimates at the provincial level. Similarly, if we want disaggregated estimates for a certain minority group within a region, such could also be considered as a small area.

Many approaches borrow strength from multiple data sources, and the choice usually depends on the parameter being estimated and data sources available. Succeeding chapters provide details on the methodology and data requirements of various SAE techniques.

1.1.1 Viewing the Disaggregated Data Requirements of the Sustainable Development Goals as a Small Area Estimation Problem

In 2000, the former prime minister of the United Kingdom, claimed that "information replaces oil as the most important commodity."[1] Information is analogous to oil: both undergo a long process of trans-formation, from crude to refined. Raw data is information in its crude form. It goes through several phases, from collection to processing and analysis to conversion to information, which is essential for evidence-based decision making. Indeed, governments increasingly recognize that data and statistics inform policy and affect development outcomes. Implementation of the MDGs further cemented the central role of timely and reliable statistics as the lifeblood of policymaking, because their specific, time-bound, and quantified targets provided a clear monitoring framework for assessing socioeconomic progress.

The MDGs achieved remarkable accomplishments. For instance, in 1990 almost 2 billion people lived on $1.25 or less a day. By 2010, fewer than 700 million people lived in extreme poverty,[2] and this figure is expected to drop to 250 million by 2030.[3] Since 1990, the number of out-of-school children of primary school age has decreased by 40 million, and almost 7 million fewer deaths occurred among children under 5 years of age.

---

[1] https://money.cnn.com/2000/01/28/europe/davos_blair/.

[2] According to estimates from the World Bank. https://www5.worldbank.org/mdgs/poverty_hunger.html.

[3] The SDGs use an updated international poverty line of $1.9 per day. In 2015, when the SDGs officially started, the World Bank estimated that 10.0% lived on less $1.9 per day.

Despite encouraging trends depicted by these aggregate-level estimates, where granular data are available, evidence suggests that the gap between rich and poor widened over time. If such inequality persists, vulnerable groups could be left out or, at best, benefit disproportionately less as the development process unfolds.

The SDGs were launched in 2015 to build on the progress achieved by the MDGs. To operationalize the SDGs, a similar indicator framework articulates specific types of data for monitoring purposes. The global indicator framework has 17 goals, 169 targets, and 231 indicators.[4] Among the global SDG indicators, 39.2% are typically collected from administrative registers, 30.6% from surveys, and 4.7% from digital sources; the remaining indicators could not be classified for different reasons (UNESCAP 2019). Whereas MDG monitoring focused on examining national-level trends, recommendations suggest disaggregating SDG indicators according to income class, gender, ethnicity, geographic location, disability status, migration status, and other relevant dimensions.[5] Potentially, the non-availability of timely and high-quality disaggregated data could render monitoring of progress toward the SDGs ineffective.

In several instances, SDG indicators can be easily disaggregated with respect to some of the dimensions specified in the global indicator framework using existing data. However, there are indicators that cannot be easily disaggregated. Figure 1.1 summarizes the findings of a survey jointly conducted by ADB and UNESCAP in 2017, which probed the availability of disaggregated SDG data among its member countries. Survey findings suggest that disaggregation of statistics by location is more widely available, however, granular data is sparse for special groups such as disabled persons and indigenous peoples. Moreover, the level of available geographical disaggregation may not be optimal for policymaking. For instance, it is possible that an indicator can be easily disaggregated by region without compromising its reliability. However, policymakers would be better informed if the same set of statistics were disaggregated at the village-level.

Given the need to strengthen the capacity of national statistical systems to compile disaggregated data for monitoring the SDGs, the UN Statistical Commission formed the Interagency Expert Group on Sustainable Development Goal Indicators.[6]

There are several ways to generate disaggregated statistics, each with its own advantages and disadvantages. Option 1 would design a data collection vehicle and ensure that there is enough (reliable) information from any desired disaggregation level. If the data collection vehicle is a survey, the process entails calculating sample size at all desired levels of disaggregation and choosing the largest sample size. As the disaggregation level becomes finer, the recommended sample size increases. Consider a hypothetical population consisting of 20 million units and spanning 17 regions and 85 provinces. Figure 1.2 shows the recommended sample size, under simple random sampling, for estimating a parameter of interest (expressed as a ratio) with a margin of error of 0.05 and a 95% confidence level based on different levels of disaggregation. This option is ideal if financial and technical resources are not an issue.

---

[4] Global indicator framework figures as of March 2020.

[5] Disaggregation is the "breakdown of observations within a common branch of a hierarchy to a more detailed level to that at which detailed observations are taken. With standard hierarchical classifications, categories can be split when finer details are required and made possible by the codes given to the primary observations." https://unstats.un.org/unsd/classifications/bestpractices/glossary_short.pdf.

[6] The Interagency Expert Group on Sustainable Development Goal Indicators' mandates are to "develop the necessary statistical standards and tools, including by establishing a working group to work on data disaggregation" and "to clearly determine the dimensions and categories of data disaggregation." https://unstats.un.org/sdgs/iaeg-sdgs/disaggregation/.

Figure 1.1: Availability of Disaggregated Data from the Sustainable Development Goals among Asian Development Bank–United Nations Economic and Social Commission for Asia and the Pacific Member Economies

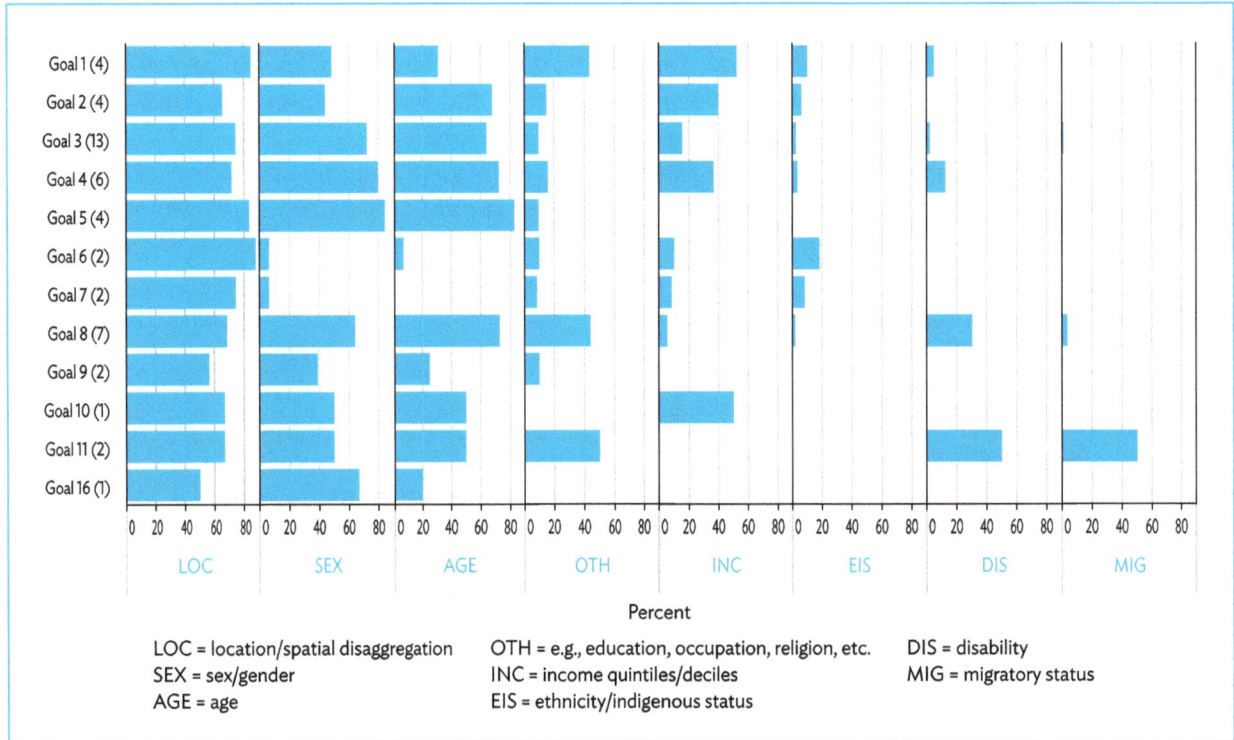

LOC = location/spatial disaggregation
SEX = sex/gender
AGE = age

OTH = e.g., education, occupation, religion, etc.
INC = income quintiles/deciles
EIS = ethnicity/indigenous status

DIS = disability
MIG = migratory status

Source: Serrao. 2017. Presentation on SDG Data Compilation: Overview of country practices related to data disaggregation in Asia and the Pacific.

Figure 1.2: Recommended Sample Size for Different Levels of Geographic Disaggregation

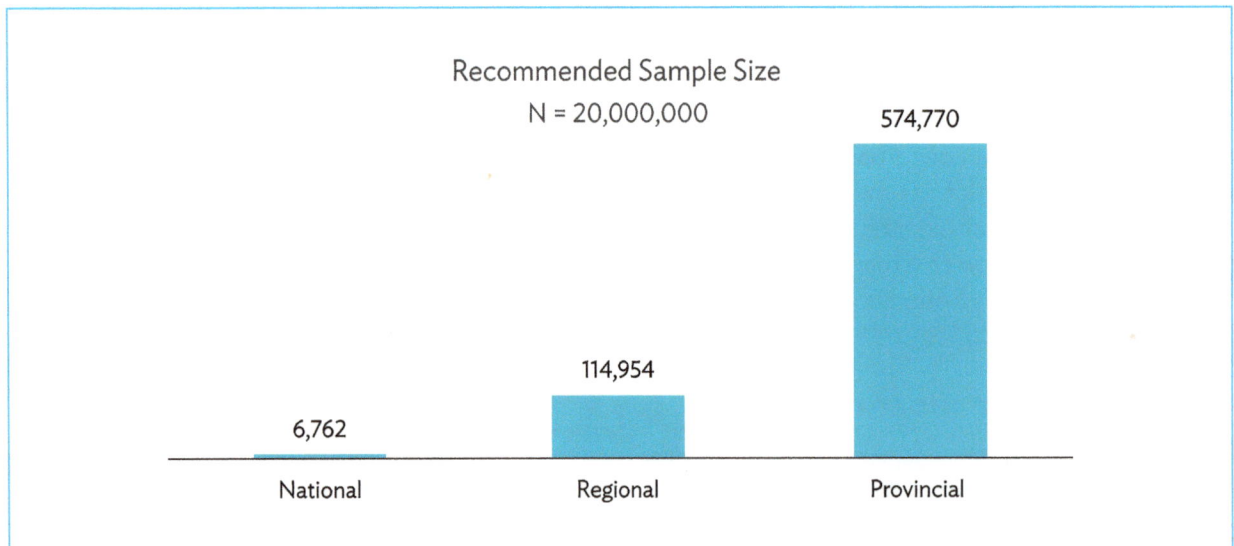

Source: Asian Development Bank estimates.

Option 2 is particularly relevant when several local-level organizations can compile official statistics. In particular, one possibility involves decentralizing data collection, within the technical supervision of NSOs, and mandating local government and/or authorities or agencies to oversee the welfare of a specific population group. If data collection follows this approach, the process will depend heavily on the budget and technical capacity of the local government authority. Some agencies may have higher resources for data collection than others, so they are in a better position to embark in such initiative. The agency may collect data in accordance with their needs, following their own schedule. However, other agencies may not be as capable (financially or technically) of doing their own data collection. Consequently, statistics will not be available for all localities or population groups. Likewise, data collection may not be synchronized (i.e., data are not simultaneously collected in all small areas because some areas are bigger compared to others). Another challenge is ensuring the adoption of consistent concepts and definitions in the data collection and analysis. This may lead to inconsistencies in data disaggregation, rendering comparability of statistics contentious.

Option 3 identifies the minimum level of disaggregation needed and designs the corresponding data collection vehicle to provide reliable estimates at that minimum level of disaggregation. For example, suppose that a national government needs reliable poverty statistics at the provincial-level, at the very least. In this case, the province is the minimum level of required disaggregation. Unlike Option 1, Option 3 is deemed more practical and cost-effective. There may be instances when only few observations are gathered for a certain subpopulation group, especially when it falls outside the prespecified minimum level of disaggregation. In our example, which identifies the province as the minimum level of required disaggregation, further disaggregation within the province may lack sufficient information or data. If the data collection vehicle is a survey, the possible consequence is a survey estimate with a high standard error and a high coefficient of variation. Anyhow, if Option 3 is considered the most practical solution under certain circumstances and a survey happens to be the main data source, exploring the feasibility of applying small area estimation to compile statistics beyond the minimum level of required disaggregation is advisable.

1.1.2   Which Sustainable Development Goal Indicators Could Benefit from Small Area Estimation?

The lack of granular or disaggregated data is not always a SAE problem. There are instances when fundamental issues remain unresolved (e.g., conceptual definitions are not available), which prevents the compilation of disaggregated data. SAE is relevant when (i) an indicator is compiled from survey data and disaggregation at a certain level is not feasible because the underlying sample size is not large enough to provide reliable estimates at that level, and (ii) there are auxiliary data sources (not prone to sampling error) from which information on the correlates of the main indicator of interest could be drawn. (On the other hand, SAE may not be relevant for indicators whose main data source is not a survey or for instances when there is no other source of auxiliary data from which we can borrow "strength" and, in turn, enhance the granularity of the survey estimates.) Thus, SDG indicators compiled by surveys could be further disaggregated when SAE is applied.

The following section reviews applications of SAE when compiling SDG indicators on poverty, employment, and health—three areas where surveys compile many indicators. SAE techniques could also be applied in other non-SDG indicators, as discussed in other local level statistics.

1.1.2.1 Poverty Statistics

SDG 1 aims to end poverty in all forms everywhere. Many indicators under this goal are compiled via surveys. Take a case where the proportion of people living below a national or international poverty line. NSOs usually generate official poverty statistics at the national, regional, and/or provincial level, using data collected from a Household Income and Expenditure Survey (HIES) or a Living Standards Measurement Survey. Often, the sample sizes of these surveys are large enough to provide reliable estimates when poverty statistics are summarized by population groups (e.g., gender, age, occupation of an individual or household head) at the national or regional level. Poverty statistics are very useful to governments when they plan, design, and monitor programs for poverty reduction if they are disaggregated by village; ethnicity in various geographic areas; or, more generally, at levels or small areas wherein the surveys were not originally designed to provide reliable estimates.

Several studies illustrate the utilization of SAE to generate disaggregated poverty statistics. A US study aiming to estimate poverty and housing unit characteristics in small areas used survey data to develop a hierarchical logistic model that included housing units and personal information (Malec 2005). In the Philippines, a growing number of studies are investigating SAE technique applications to poverty. At the subnational level, SAE of poverty was initially studied in 1999, when synthetic estimation procedure was applied in the Family Income and Expenditure Survey (FIES) and Census of Population and Housing (CPH) data to estimate poverty incidence at the provincial or city level (Albacea 1999). In 2003, this procedure was modified to generate provincial poverty estimates (Albacea and Pacificador 2003). Both studies led to the proposed procedure for estimating local poverty statistics in the Philippines (Albacea 2006). In 2007, another application of SAE technique measured the incidence of food poverty in provincial agricultural and fisheries households, using three estimation procedures (i.e., direct, regression-synthetic, and empirical best linear unbiased prediction) on data from survey, census, and administrative sources (Cosico 2007). In response to demands for more geographically disaggregated poverty statistics, the National Statistical Coordination Board (now part of the Philippine Statistics Authority) generated municipal- and city-level poverty statistics, using the World Bank methodology commonly referred to as Elbers, Lanjouw and Lanjouw (ELL) methodology. Other studies in the Philippines used different SAE techniques to estimate the number of poor households in municipalities and cities within a region (Bulan 2011; Yuson 2012; Alcanices 2013; Bernasol 2013; Caisido 2013; and De Guzman 2013). Thailand uses ELL methodology to generate district and subdistrict poverty indicators using CPH and the Household Socio-Economic Survey.[7]

Box 1.1 further discusses SAE of poverty statistics in Philippines and Thailand, two Asian countries that integrate SAE into their regular work programs.

---

[7] The use of Big Data in estimating local poverty statistics is currently gaining attention among researchers. As reported in UN Global Pulse, a proxy indicator of poverty in Uganda was developed based on the roofing materials as captured in satellite images for a particular district of Gulu in 2012 (https://www.uneca.org/sites/default/files/uploaded-documents/ACS/SR-BIGDATA-GEOSPATIAL-SDG-2018/session3-uganda-harnessing_big_data_for_statistical_purposes_in_uganda_april_23-25_2018.pdf). Likewise, consumption expenditure and asset wealth were estimated using high-resolution survey- and satellite data-based imagery from five African countries (i.e., Nigeria, Tanzania, Uganda, Malawi and Rwanda). Although the estimation was calculated at the country level, the country was considered part of a larger area (i.e., the African Region). Jean, et al. reported in 2016 that the data used in this estimation are the nighttime lights and daytime satellite images which are classified as Big Data.

Box 1.1: Small Area Estimation of Poverty in the Philippines and Thailand

Philippines

The Philippine Statistics Authority (PSA) compiles the official poverty statistics for the country. PSA reported that 16.6% of the population in 2018, or about one in every six Filipinos, lived below the national poverty line. The PSA generates poverty statistics at the national, regional, provincial and highly urbanized city levels estimated directly from the triennial Family Income and Expenditure Survey (FIES).

Recognizing the clamor for more granular poverty estimates at the subnational level, the PSA embarked on a Poverty Mapping Project with the World Bank in 2005. The project's main outputs are small area poverty estimates for all the municipalities and cities in the country for the year 2000. The PSA subsequently produced small area estimates of poverty for 2003, 2006, and 2009 through several projects initially funded by the World Bank, and the Government of Australia. Recognizing the importance of generating lower level statistics on poverty, the Government of the Philippines fully funded the 2012 and the 2015 projects on the generation of the city and municipal level estimates resulting to the release of the 2012 and 2015 poverty estimates for municipalities and cities in the country. As of this writing, the small area estimation of poverty has not yet been adopted by the Philippine Statistical System as part of official statistics, although this statistical activity is included in the Philippine Statistical Development Program, which contains priority statistical development programs and activities designed to ensure the availability of crucial information for national development planning and international commitments.

In the Philippines, municipal- and city-level poverty estimates have been very useful for evidence-based economic and social policies and programs for poverty reduction. Additionally, such estimates are widely used by national and local government units as well as international organizations. The Department of Social Welfare and Development used this information to identify poor municipalities and those with pockets of poverty for the first and second phases of the National Household Targeting System for Poverty Reduction data collection. These data guided the classification and updating of target beneficiaries for the Pantawid Pamilya Pilipino Program, a flagship anti-poverty program of the Government of the Philippines.

SAEs also help identify local government recipients of some internationally and locally funded projects.[a] Additionally, municipal- and city-level poverty estimates provide inputs for socioeconomic profiles and reports in Negros Occidental and Pangasinan provinces; Nabas in Aklan province; and Baguio City and La Trinidad, Itogon, Sablan and Tuba municipalities in Benguet. Estimates also served as the basis for formulating and assessing the implementation of poverty reduction programs in Aklan, La Union, Negros Occidental, Pangasinan, and Southern Leyte provinces (PSA 2013 and 2016).

Thailand

The National Economic and Social Development Board (NESDB) compiles national, regional, and provincial poverty statistics, while the National Statistical Office (NSO) generates district and subdistrict poverty statistics. Based on the latest NESDB statistics (2017), about 7.87% of Thailand's population is poor.

Thailand halved its poor population far ahead of the Millennium Development Goals' 2015 deadline. However, poverty reduction varies across different geographical areas. Therefore, Thailand shifted its intervention priorities to smaller geographical areas with pockets of poverty (Jitsuchon and Richter 2007). To achieve this goal, the NESDB and NSO collaborated with the Thailand Development Research Institute and the World Bank to develop poverty maps based on SAE methodology in 2003. Succeeding SAEs of poverty for 2005, 2007, 2009, 2011, 2013, 2015 and 2017 are replicated by the NESDB and NSO.

continued on next page

Box 1.1 *continued*

SAEs of poverty are essential tools for eradicating poverty in Thailand. The estimates serve as inputs for assessing poverty, inequality, and other economic and social problems, and also help evaluate poverty-related policies and develop local poverty reduction strategies. In particular, SAEs provide evidence in formulating policy on developing quality of life for people with state welfare cards. It also serves as a basis for the government's child support grant, which provides a subsidy for newborn babies in families or households classified as poor or at risk of being poor.

---

[a] Projects include Panay Island Sustainable Agricultural Upland Development Projects in the municipalities of Alimodian in Iloilo, Tapaz and Jamindan in Capiz, Libacao in Aklan, and Patnongon in Antique; Philippine Rural Development Project funded by the World Bank in collaboration with the local government and the private sector in Western Visayas; and World Food Programme and Department of Social Welfare and Development assistance to families affected by typhoon Yolanda (Haiyan) in Western Visayas. Further, the estimates are used as basis in targeting beneficiaries for the United Nations Children's Fund (UNICEF), United Nations Population Fund, the Early Childhood Care and Development Council, PLAN Philippines, Philippine National Red Cross/Agencia Espanola de Cooperacion Internacionale, Department of Agriculture/ADB Infrastructure for Rural Productivity Enhancement Sector Project and German Technical Cooperation Livelihood Programs and Projects in Eastern Samar; and National Community Driven Development Program in Central Visayas Region. The estimates are also utilized by the Student Grants-in-Aid Program for Poverty Alleviation in the Cordillera Administrative Region; Cash-for-Training Program in the Soccsksargen Region; and Kapit Bisig Laban sa Kahirapan-Comprehensive and Integrated Delivery of Social Services Program in Manila, Cavite, Bicol Region, Negros Oriental, and Butuan City.

Sources: Philippine Statistics Authority (PSA). 2016. *2012 Municipal and City Level Poverty Estimates*. Manila; PSA. 2013. *2006 and 2009 Municipal and City Level Poverty Estimates*. Manila.; Jitsuchon, S. and K. Richter. 2007. Chapter 13 Thailand's Poverty Maps: From Construction to Application. *Thailand Northeast Economic Development Report.*; and Sangaroon, B., Kaew-Amdee, T. and B. Khananurak. 2019. *Presentation on Small Area Estimation Method and Big Data*. International Workshop on Data Disaggregation for the SDGs. Bangkok, Thailand.

1.1.2.2 Employment Statistics

The SDGs also aim to promote full and productive employment and decent work for all women and men, including young people and persons with disabilities, and equal pay for equal work. The Labor Force Survey, which follows a common international framework of the International Labour Organization, collects data about labor and employment statistics. Similar to poverty statistics, labor, employment, and decent work statistics are relevant for government policymaking and program planning, not just nationally and regionally but also at smaller geographical levels, which use surveys not originally designed to provide reliable estimates.

Several studies show how SAE methods aid the production of granular-level employment indicators. In the Philippines, a study combines nationwide survey and census data with administrative data to generate the provincial unemployment rate among women and youth (Victoria 2008). Similarly, SAE technique is applied when estimating the total number of unemployed persons in municipalities and cities within a region (Lauan 2010) or province (Borromeo 2011). Meanwhile, the SAE approach is used to estimate the total number of employed persons at the municipal and city level of a region, categorized by highest educational attainment (Doctolero 2015) and major industry (De los Reyes 2015). Using a model-based SAE approach, the proportion of households with members classified as working children aged 5–17 years is also estimated at the regional level (Julongbayan 2017).

1.1.2.3   Health and Nutrition Statistics

SDG 3 aims to ensure healthy lives and promote well-being for people of all ages. Under this goal, most indicators are compiled via surveys or administrative data sources. Health and nutrition statistics are collected through the Demographic and Health Surveys, the Multiple Indicators and Cluster Survey, and administrative sources from health ministries and national and local, public and private health institutions.

Several studies combine different data collection vehicles to measure a more granular level of health and nutrition statistics. In the United States, a study applied the SAE method to the Behavioral Risk Factor Surveillance System data set in 1999–2005 to obtain the prevalence of obesity in 398 communities in the Commonwealth of Massachusetts (Li, Kelsey and Zhang 2009). Similarly, the prevalence of childhood obesity was measured through SAE technique using data from the National Survey of Children's Health (Zhang, Onufrak, Holt and Croft 2013). Three SAE methods were assessed to generate county-level health indicators in the country (Chien, Lin, Li and Zhang 2018). Meanwhile, logistic regression was applied to data from the National Hospital Ambulatory Medical Care Survey and also from counties and hospitals to generate the proportions of emergency department indicators (i.e., ambulance arrival rates, asthma-related visits, and injury-related visits) (Beresovsky, Burt, Parsons and Schenker 2010).

In the Philippines, a study combined data from the National Nutrition Survey, the census, and administrative sources to estimate the proportion of underweight children aged 0–5 years in provinces (Sotto 2006) and villages (Amar 2007). Likewise, SAE techniques were implemented to measure other nutrition indicators, the proportion of stunted children aged 0–5 years in the provinces (Castillo, Molano and Albacea 2007), and the number of wasted children aged 0–5 years in municipalities and cities within a region (Amiscosa 2010). Other notable SAE applications include estimating the number of underweight children aged 0–5 years in municipalities and cities in two different regions (Relente 2010 and Aracid 2014), the proportion of underweight children aged 0–5 years in all cities and municipalities nationwide (Arlan 2016), and the proportion of Vitamin A-deficient children aged 6 months–5 years in the provinces (Abitona 2011). Meanwhile, occurences of maternal mortality, which is a difficult-to-measure SDG indicator, was estimated using Poisson regression models in cities and municipalities within a region (Nuestro 2014) or province.

In Italy, a study applied Poisson regression to the Health Conditions and Appeal to Medical Survey data to obtain the average number of visits by people aged 65 years or older to district physicians within the past four weeks in Liguria, Toscana, and Umbria (Tzvidis, Rannali, Salvati, Dreassi and Chambers 2013). In Australia, local disability statistics were generated and compared using three estimation models (i.e., demographic synthetic, Poisson, and Bernoulli) (Elazar and Conn 2004).

1.1.2.4   Other Local Statistics

SAE techniques can also be applied in other fields (e.g., agriculture, forestry, education). A study developed regression models to measure the number of households engaged in nonfarming activities in Cauvery Command Area villages in India (Sudhakar 2009). Another research work used logistic regression models to generate mean proportion forest coverage in Northern Minnesota in the United States (McRoberts 2010). Meanwhile, a study in the Republic of Korea applied model based SAE technique to incorporate the spatial information of local areas in proportion estimates (Shim and Hwang 2016). In Senegal, another application of the SAE method combined data from conventional sources with Big Data (i.e., survey data and mobile phone data) to estimate literacy rates for men and women at the district level (Schmid, Burckschen, Salvati and Zbiranski 2017). A Philippine study used SAE procedure to determine the proportion of households that think there is a serious drug abuse problem in the community at the regional level (Gliponeo 2017).

This chapter has provided a gentle introduction on applications of SAE, particularly in the context of meeting the disaggregated data requirements of the SDGs. Before we discuss different methods of small area estimation, we turn to the next chapter, which reviews the different components of SAE action plan.

CHAPTER II

DEVELOPING A SMALL AREA ESTIMATION PLAN

In the previous chapter, we discussed the concept of SAE and explored how this technique can enhance the granularity of survey estimates by disaggregating them at levels for which the underlying survey was not originally designed. Like many other statistical activities, it is important to develop an implementation plan before embarking on SAE. Most of the following discussion focuses on the practical aspects and considerations deemed important for NSO technical staff. Nevertheless, most considerations covered in this chapter may also apply to other, more general contexts that confront students, academe, and other types of researchers who wish to conduct SAE. On the other hand, readers who prefer a more theoretical discussion could supplement this guide with SAE textbooks and other references.[8]

As the literature and applications of SAE flourish, the list of methodologies abounds. There is a wide array of SAE techniques: some are easy to apply, while others are more challenging. Other factors include the purpose or objective for conducting SAE, type of indicator or variable of interest, and availability of data prior to the actual estimation.

2.1 Goal or Purpose of Small Area Estimation

The main objective of generating granular or disaggregated statistics should be clear before embarking on any SAE activity. Granular estimates should be generated only when there is a valid clamor for such statistics and when no other proxy data at the small area level are available for use in policymaking and program planning. Additionally, we should assess whether there is an insignificant difference between small areas, and whether broad area level estimates or part of broad area level estimates would suffice. NSOs collect voluminous data and compile data based on those inputs. Statistical data collection activities require considerable financial and technical resources, so embarking on another statistical activity could potentially strain their limited resources. SAE could be a very complex exercise that entails thorough validation of the estimates. Hence, ensuring an efficient allocation of resources will require a demand for the outputs of SAE.

Chapter I cites several examples of how outputs of small area estimation were used for policy planning and design, particularly in the Philippines and Thailand. In many instances, these uses need to be articulated right from the start of NSO planning of priority statistical activities. If potential uses of any statistical activity are not clear at the outset, mobilizing budget may prove to be a very difficult task.

However, data producers like NSOs do not always know how compiled statistics are being used, what types of additional data are needed, and other requirements of socioeconomic planners. Importantly,

---

[8] A good reference is a paper entitled *"Small Area Estimation: An Appraisal"* written by Ghosh and Rao published in the journal *"Statistical Science"* in 1994. This article was expanded into a book, *Small Area Estimation* by Rao to cover the different SAE techniques and its applications prior to 2003. More applications using different forms of models and comparing different SAE methodologies could be seen in recent literature. Some applications and studies conducted after 2003 are provided in this handbook and grouped according to the indicator being measured at the disaggregated level.

NSOs must reach out and consult their key stakeholders. A guide published by the Australian Bureau of Statistics (2006) provides a checklist of questions to ask key stakeholders prior to SAE exercises:

- What are the important policies or programs that potentially require granular data?
- What are the users/stakeholders' strategic context, goals and desired results?
- What specific granular data do users require and what geographic or subpopulation level is needed?
- What are the corresponding effects on the policies or programs if the reference granular data is inaccurate, e.g., by 5%, 10%, or 20%? Which granular data should be prioritized with respect to accuracy requirements?
- Are there available social or economic models that can serve as reference in identifying the potential variables for explaining the variable of interest?
- What are the relevant administrative-level data that can serve as additional information for the small area model? How are these data gathered, what are their uses and what are their level of accuracy?
- Will the granular estimates be further disaggregated to other geographic or subpopulation categories?
- What are the available literatures that discuss the corresponding policies or programs which utilize the granular estimates?

Knowing the key policies, funding decisions, or questions that disaggregated statistics can address is essential when developing an SAE implementation plan. Because different stakeholders may need varying disaggregated data, consultations are also useful in identifying whose data needs can be addressed most efficiently by conducting SAE. SAE is not a simple solution that can address all disaggregated data requirements of every user. Therefore, consultation is a good opportunity to communicate the limitations of SAE to target users.

2.2 Variable of Interest

When developing an SAE implementation plan, it is also important to carefully examine the characteristics of the variable of interest. The variable of interest is usually estimated from NSOs' sample survey. Suppose we want to compile small area poverty statistics and the proportion of poor population (i.e., the variable of interest) is constant across large geographic areas, then we do not need auxiliary information to build a model. A simple estimation procedure (e.g., the broad area ratio estimator) would suffice. Nevertheless, in reality this technique entails a strong assumption. However, if the proportion of poor is believed to be different across small geographic areas, we can proceed with obtaining auxiliary data to build a model.

When compiling small area poverty estimates, we must specify whether we need estimates of headcount poverty rates only, or we also need estimates of other types of poverty indicators (e.g., poverty gap, poverty severity). This type of technical question must be answered early, because the choice of SAE methodology depends on the form of the variable of interest.

A variable may assume different forms (e.g., a sum, average, proportion or ratio). If the underlying population size is known, the headcount poverty rate or poverty incidence may be considered as a proportion or average of a binary variable that takes a value of one if the observation unit is considered poor or zero if non-poor. If the underlying population size is unknown, headcount poverty rate may be considered as a ratio. Unemployment and underemployment rates are also considered as ratio. On the other hand, the total number of poor people and total number of unemployed are expressed as sum.

Importantly, some SAE methodologies are applicable to one form of variable, but not to others. If small area estimates are needed for variables of different forms, using different SAE methodology for each variable of interest may be considered.

2.3   Level of Disaggregation and Data Requirements

Following the definition provided in Chapter I, a small area could be either a geographical unit or a subpopulation group that is not adequately represented in the underlying survey because it is finer than the pre-specified survey domain and because of limitations in sample size. The desired level of disaggregation is usually dictated by the goal or purpose of conducting SAE. This should align with the users' requirements for policy decisions and program implementation. For practical reasons, disaggregation is usually set at the lower administrative regions.

In some instances, data producers publish direct survey estimates at the small area-level, but with caveats for small areas where the corresponding direct survey estimates fall below a pre-specified reliability threshold. This is a common practice, especially when there are very few small areas whose direct survey estimates have low levels of reliability. SAE becomes more appealing when many units of the desired level of disaggregation have direct survey estimates falling below a pre-specified reliability threshold. However, conducting SAE does not guarantee substantially higher levels of reliability at any desired level of disaggregation than direct survey estimation. The choice of SAE methodology hinges on the level at which additional information is available.

SAE techniques are valuable when they can capitalize on additional information, which can explain the innate relationships within and between the survey data and other sources of data. These relationships can be drawn within and between different possible sources: between direct survey estimates and auxiliary data from administrative sources, censuses, or other surveys; between direct survey estimates generated over time; in information collected between adjacent small areas; between units sharing the same features in various small areas within one large area; or combinations of the sources mentioned. However, drawing strength from some of these sources could complicate SAE, thus requiring statistical expertise.

The availability of auxiliary data that could potentially explain the variable of interest is one of the most important requirements of SAE. Auxiliary data may be available at area-level or person/unit level or both. When choosing auxiliary data, quality checks can be done on concepts, definitions, standard classifications, scope, mode of data collection, purpose of data collection, questionnaire and methodology used for data collection, sampling design (if survey), reference periods, missing data, and data validation can be used to anticipate the limitations of the SAE model. Previous or related studies may be used as reference. Testing the strength and significance of the relationship between the auxiliary data and the variable(s) of interest is imperative. This could be done through simple scatter plots, correlation, and simple models. Further, it is important that auxiliary data (i) cover the whole population where small area estimates will be generated, (ii) include required geographic or subpopulation information, and (iii) have a consistent reference period with the variable(s) of interest and other auxiliary data.

Administrative data is one source of auxiliary data. However, consistency of the definitions used in the collection of these data must be checked. For example, the social welfare office and a statistics office may define a poor household differently. The quality of administrative data should be assessed depending on the quality of data collection procedure implemented. Moreover, there is no way to measure the error in using this type of data in the estimation procedure.

Recently, more data are derived from internet resources and industry. Social media and even satellites provide enormous data. These sources provide real-time data known as Big Data. Utilizing these data in SAE provides an alternative way of generating estimates. Although issues of bias of social media data still prevent its actual use, ongoing research on methodologies can address these problems. On the other hand, issues of confidentiality haunt the use of data from mobile phone providers and sales of medicine. Despite these issues, some recent studies explore big data as a potential source of auxiliary data.

2.4 Approach to Small Area Estimation and Choosing a Specific Technique or Model

The last two questions pertain to approach. A "direct approach" uses observations for the small area or small domain that were gathered from a nationwide survey, whereas an "indirect approach" uses observations and auxiliary data in mathematical and statistical models. Such models provide the functional relationship between the data obtained directly from the nationwide survey and a set of auxiliary data.

Generally, SAE models are classified into two types: simple small area models and regression-based models. Simple small area models are mostly mathematical models that use an auxiliary variable in addition to the variable of interest. The relationship is established using an arithmetic operation. Statistical models are more appropriate for estimation when several auxiliary variables are used with a random error component.

2.5 Quality Assessment of Small Area Estimates

Part of the estimation process involves checking the quality of the statistics being generated. Two levels of assessment can assure the quality of the estimates: (i) internal, or within the team doing the estimation, and (ii) external, with prospective users of the statistics or other experts.

In an internal assessment, it is necessary to evaluate the models used in the estimation. One part of model evaluation is checking whether the data satisfies the assumptions of the models. Because each model has its own set of assumptions, failure to satisfy the assumptions leads to invalid results. For example, the classical linear model has several assumptions, including that

- the relationship of the variable of interest and predictors is linear;
- predictors are fixed or measured with negligible error;
- predictors are noncollinear (i.e., there is no multi-collinearity among the predictors); and
- random errors are uncorrelated and have a common variance. In some cases, the errors are also assumed to follow the normal distribution.

These assumptions must be satisfied to justify the use of a linear model. If there is a violation, users can apply remedial measures or employ another type of model for estimation.

Model evaluation also involves looking at the adequacy (i.e., goodness of fit) of the model to the data set. Although several measures can evaluate model adequacy, the most common measure is the adjusted coefficient of determination (adjusted R^2). Another evaluation method is the chi-square goodness of fit test. Moreover, the model should possess the following characteristics:

- the signs of the coefficients can be explained logically;
- the relationship observed between the variable of interest and a predictor is supported by some theories or known concepts in the subject matter;
- the model is parsimonious (i.e., includes only relevant predictors); and
- the use of the model in prediction is cost-efficient, specifically regarding data collection.

After the models generate the small area statistics, the properties of those statistics must be evaluated, including measures of precision, accuracy, and reliability. Precision measures the closeness of the estimates to each other, whereas accuracy measures the closeness of the estimates to the true value of the parameter being estimated. The variance of the estimate or its positive square root, which is commonly called standard error of the estimate, is a measure of precision and the bias is a measure of accuracy. A combined measure of precision and accuracy is the mean square error. All of these measures should be small in value to declare that the estimates are precise and accurate. Box 2.1 further explains the difference between accuracy and precision with respect to survey sampling. On the other hand, a measure of reliability is given by the coefficient of variation that gives a measure of variability relative to the value of the estimate. Roughly, an estimate with a coefficient of variation less than 10% is reliable, whereas estimates with a very high coefficient of variation (i.e., greater than 20%) are unreliable.

Box 2.1: Difference Between Accuracy and Precision in Survey Sampling

Accuracy and precision are two important concepts in survey sampling. But what is the difference between these concepts, and which is more important? Accuracy measures how closely your sample statistics agree with mean population values. In other words, the closer your estimates are to the true population values, the more accurate the estimates. Meanwhile, precision measures the closeness of your sample statistics to each other. The closer each estimate is to the other estimates, the more precise your estimate. Both accuracy and precision should be the objective in any sampling procedure.

For instance, the bullseye in following illustration represents the mean population values and the shots are the estimates. The shots in the first diagram are neither accurate nor precise, because the holes are neither uniformly distributed over the target nor clustered together. In the second diagram, the uniformity of distribution is accurate but not precise. The third diagram shows precise shots, because the holes are close to each other, but they are not very accurate. The fourth diagram shows shots that are both accurate and precise.

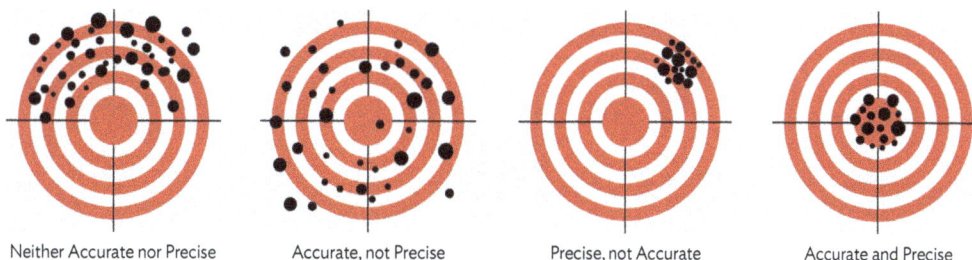

Neither Accurate nor Precise   Accurate, not Precise   Precise, not Accurate   Accurate and Precise

Source: https://commons.wikimedia.org/wiki/File:Reliability_and_validity.svg.

An external assessment of small area statistics is conducted with end users of the estimates. The stakeholders may include experts, prospective users of statistics, and even those who provided the data used in the estimation. An assessment can be done through a consultation (e.g., focus group discussion) with the stakeholders. A consultation aims to assess the applicability of the estimates and to make final adjustments prior to dissemination. Alternatively, external assessment could involve an ocular visit or direct verification. Currently, there is still no standard way to conduct an external assessment of the estimates because there is no way to verify whether the estimates themselves are correct. Ultimately, one must rely on the fact that the statistical techniques will provide estimates that minimize the chance of error.

2.6 Dissemination Strategy for Presentation of the Small Area Estimates

The last component of a SAE plan involves devising a dissemination strategy. This requires (i) knowing the target audience (i.e., users, policy makers, or researchers), and (ii) determining the best communication vehicle.

The form of dissemination depends on the target audience. An appropriate form of communication for a wider audience is a short note or online infographics on the statistics. An online presentation is more appropriate for users and researchers who want to ask questions or clarify issues regarding the estimates. The dissemination strategy is important to completing the SAE process because it allows fuller appreciation and use of exercise outputs.

In summary, a plan of action for SAE has six components:

1. Goal or Purpose of SAE
2. Form of the Variable of Interest
3. Level of Disaggregation and Data Requirements
4. SAE Approach to Use
5. Quality Assessment of the Estimates
6. Dissemination Strategy

Identifying these components and answering the guide questions lead to having a set of useful statistics.

III | DATA MANAGEMENT USING R

R and RStudio are free and open-sourced tools for data analysis. This chapter introduces the fundamentals of R, including the basics of data manipulation with codes implemented in RStudio. Readers who are interested in replicating the data exercises shown in this chapter can download and install R and RStudio on their respective computers and download the data sets online.

3.1 Overview of R and RStudio

R is a free and open-sourced programming language that is widely used by statisticians and researchers. One of the most comprehensive statistical analysis tools, R incorporates all standard statistical tests and models and provides a wide array of commands for managing and manipulating data.

RStudio is the most commonly used integrated development environment for R. This application suite allows users to interact with R more readily by integrating different aspects of scripting, from code completion to debugging.

R and RStudio are available for different operating systems. Installers can be downloaded from their respective project websites. For RStudio to function properly, install R first.

To install R, visit https://cran.r-project.org/ and select the appropriate download link (Figure 3.1). Once the installer has been downloaded, follow the screen prompts during installation.

Next, visit https://www.rstudio.com/products/rstudio/download/ to download and install RStudio. Scroll down the page to the Installers for Supported Platforms section and select the appropriate download link (Figure 3.2). Follow the screen prompts during installation.

Figure 3.1: Graphical User Interface for Downloading R

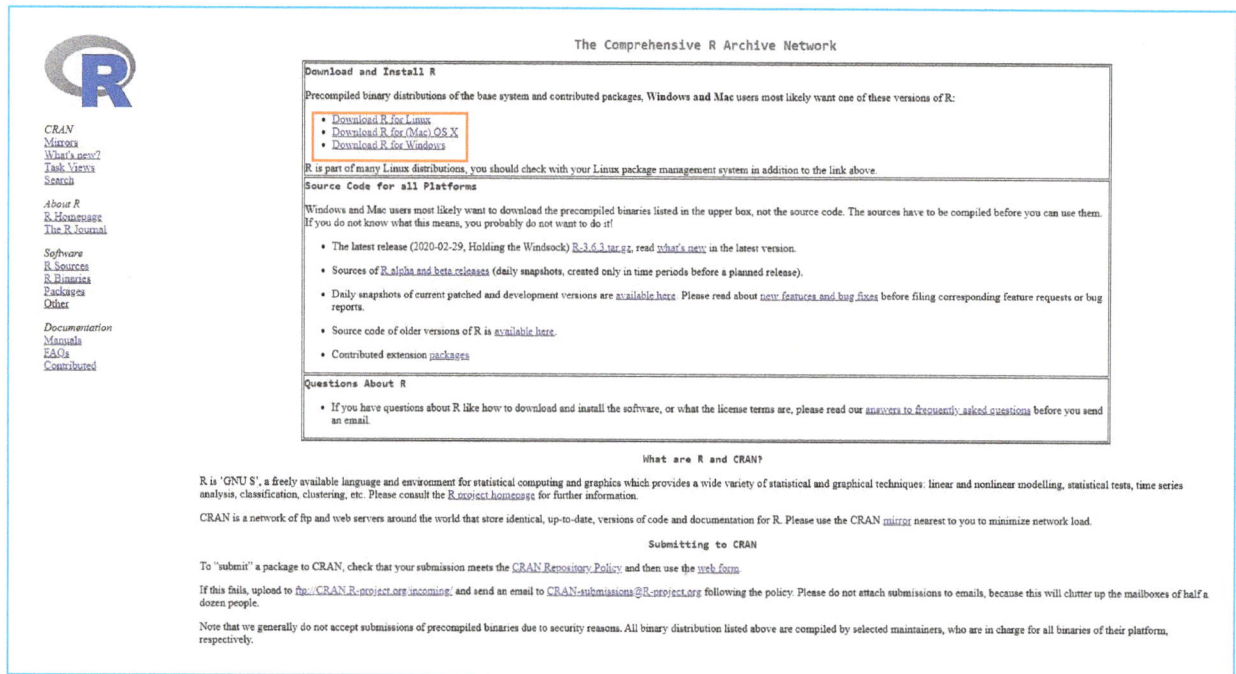

Source: Authors' screenshot of RStudio.

Figure 3.2: Installing RStudio

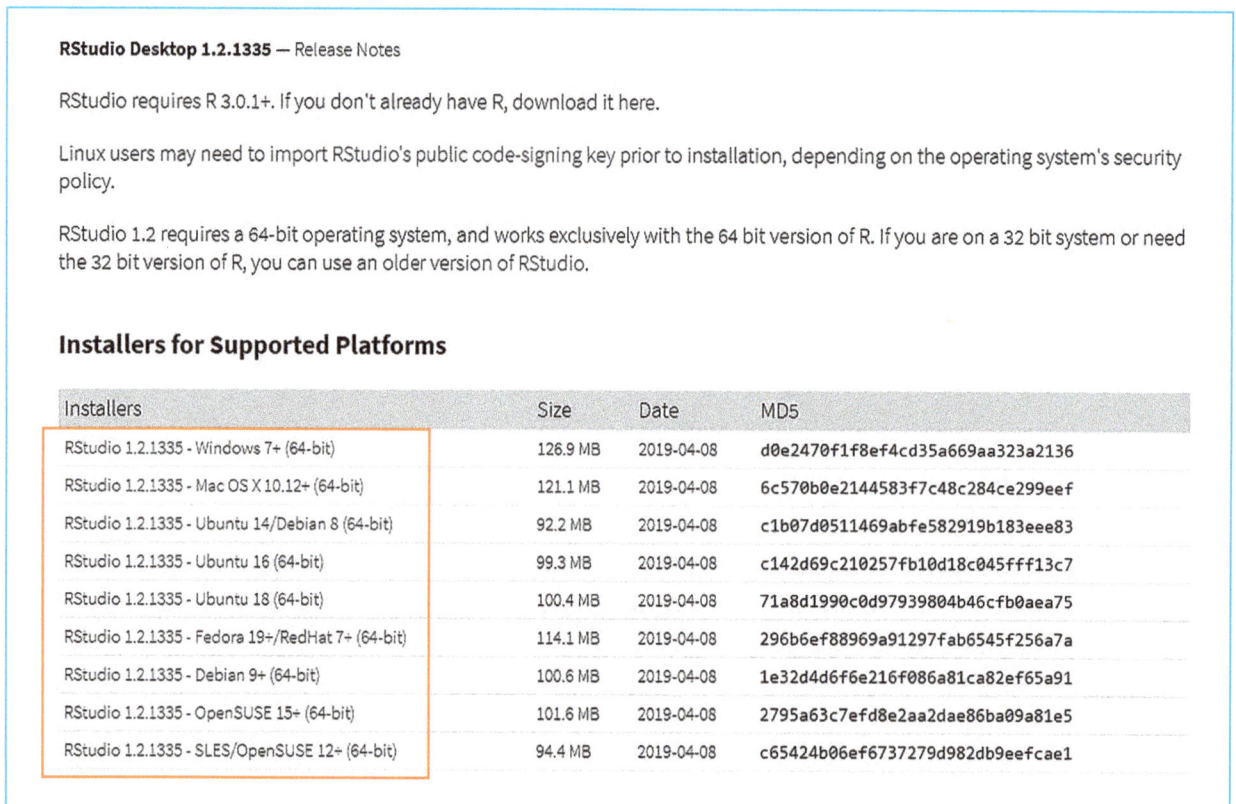

RStudio Desktop 1.2.1335 — Release Notes

RStudio requires R 3.0.1+. If you don't already have R, download it here.

Linux users may need to import RStudio's public code-signing key prior to installation, depending on the operating system's security policy.

RStudio 1.2 requires a 64-bit operating system, and works exclusively with the 64 bit version of R. If you are on a 32 bit system or need the 32 bit version of R, you can use an older version of RStudio.

Installers for Supported Platforms

Installers	Size	Date	MD5
RStudio 1.2.1335 - Windows 7+ (64-bit)	126.9 MB	2019-04-08	d0e2470f1f8ef4cd35a669aa323a2136
RStudio 1.2.1335 - Mac OS X 10.12+ (64-bit)	121.1 MB	2019-04-08	6c570b0e2144583f7c48c284ce299eef
RStudio 1.2.1335 - Ubuntu 14/Debian 8 (64-bit)	92.2 MB	2019-04-08	c1b07d0511469abfe582919b183eee83
RStudio 1.2.1335 - Ubuntu 16 (64-bit)	99.3 MB	2019-04-08	c142d69c210257fb10d18c045fff13c7
RStudio 1.2.1335 - Ubuntu 18 (64-bit)	100.4 MB	2019-04-08	71a8d1990c0d97939804b46cfb0aea75
RStudio 1.2.1335 - Fedora 19+/RedHat 7+ (64-bit)	114.1 MB	2019-04-08	296b6ef88969a91297fab6545f256a7a
RStudio 1.2.1335 - Debian 9+ (64-bit)	100.6 MB	2019-04-08	1e32d4d6f6e216f086a81ca82ef65a91
RStudio 1.2.1335 - OpenSUSE 15+ (64-bit)	101.6 MB	2019-04-08	2795a63c7efd8e2aa2dae86ba09a81e5
RStudio 1.2.1335 - SLES/OpenSUSE 12+ (64-bit)	94.4 MB	2019-04-08	c65424b06ef6737279d982db9eefcae1

Source: Authors' screenshot of RStudio.

3.1.1 The RStudio Interface

When opening RStudio for the first time, only three panels are visible. To open the fourth panel, go to File > New File > R Script, or press Ctrl + Shift + N on the keyboard (Figure 3.3).

Figure 3.3: Opening the Fourth Panel of RStudio

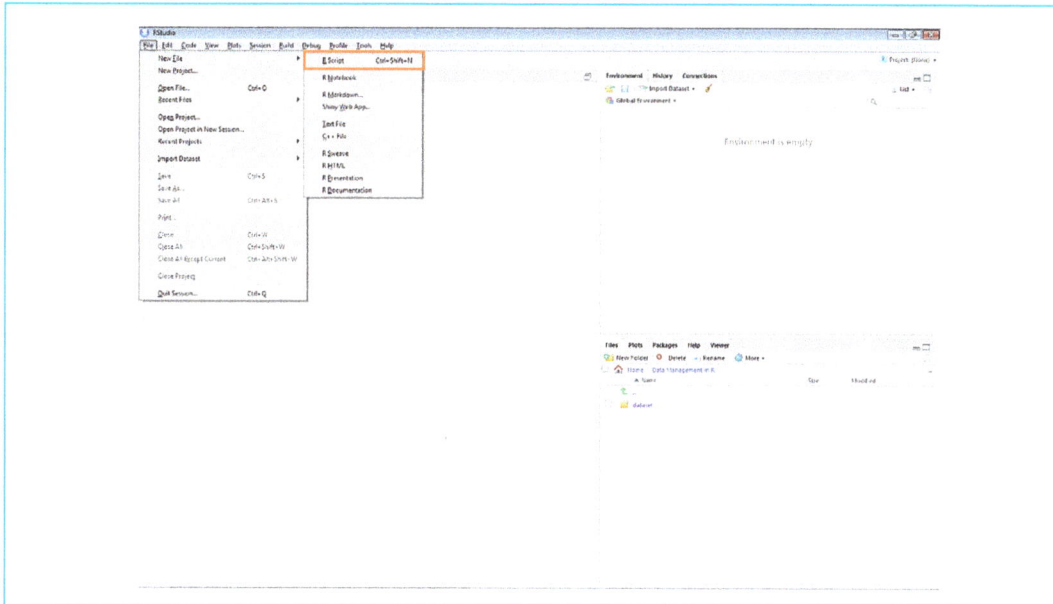

Source: Authors' screenshot of RStudio.

RStudio includes four main panels (Figure 3.4).

Figure 3.4: Four Main Panels of RStudio

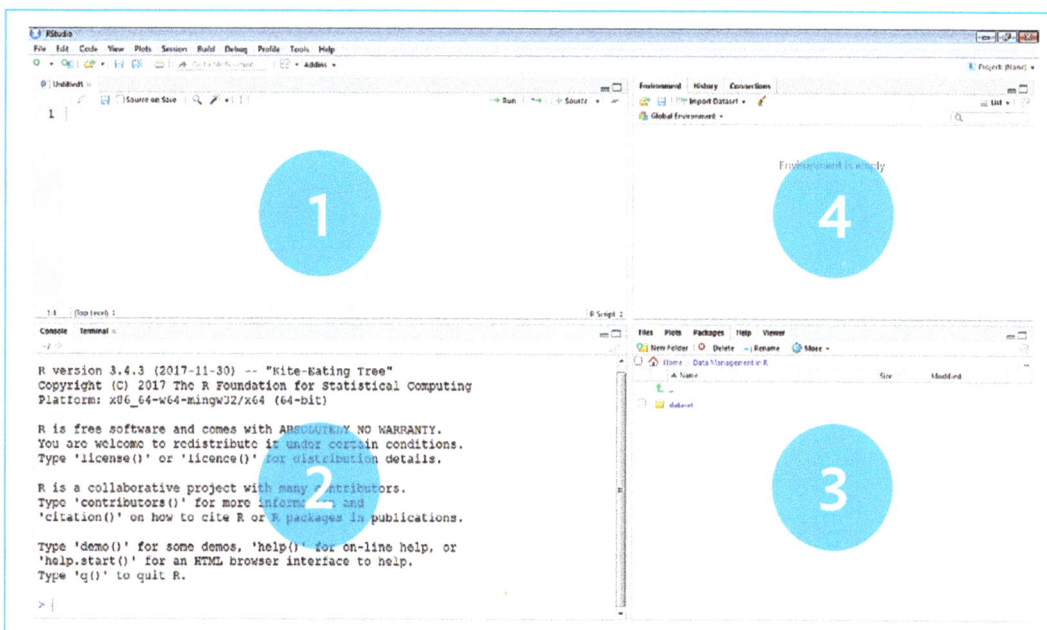

Source: Authors' screenshot of RStudio.

Panel 1 is the Editor window, where users can type, execute, and save commands and scripts. It contains navigation and scripting tools for efficient coding and debugging (Figure 3.5).

Figure 3.5: Shortcut Tools of the Editor Window in RStudio

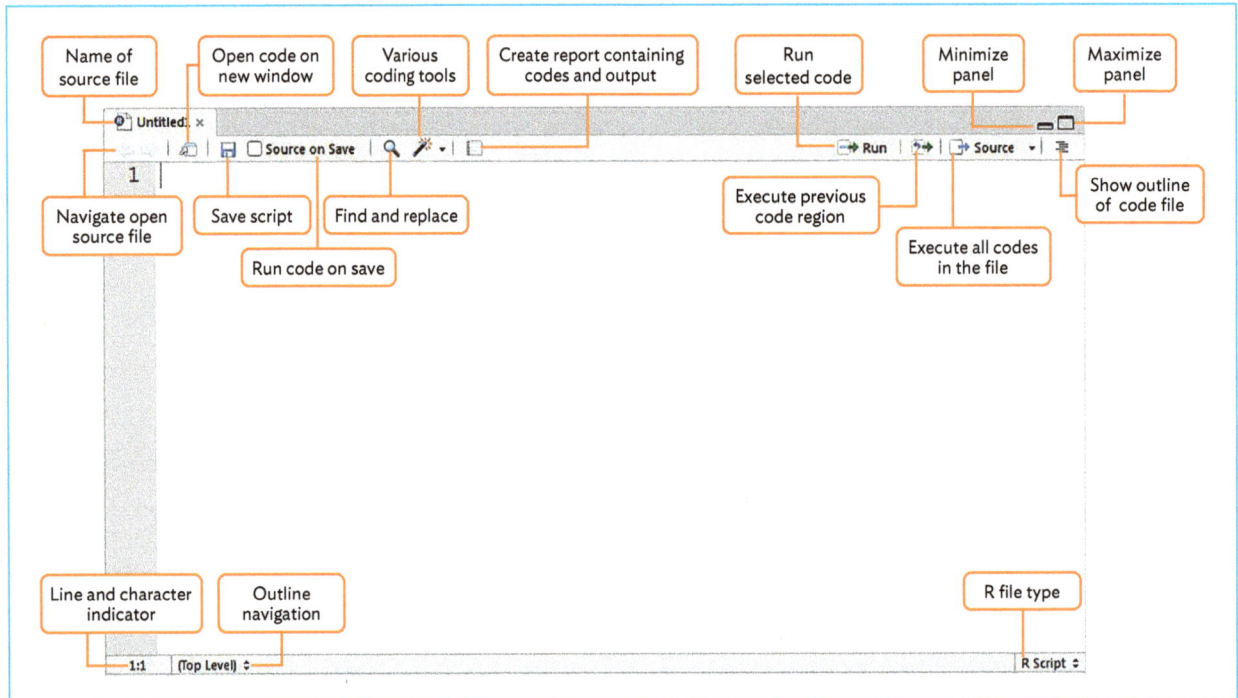

Source: Authors' screenshot of RStudio.

Panel 2 is the Console window, which displays the output from running codes in the Editor window (Figure 3.6). Simpler commands and one-line codes may be executed in Panel 2. The Console window also displays the current working directory of RStudio and identifies the version of R currently in use.

Figure 3.6: Console Window in RStudio

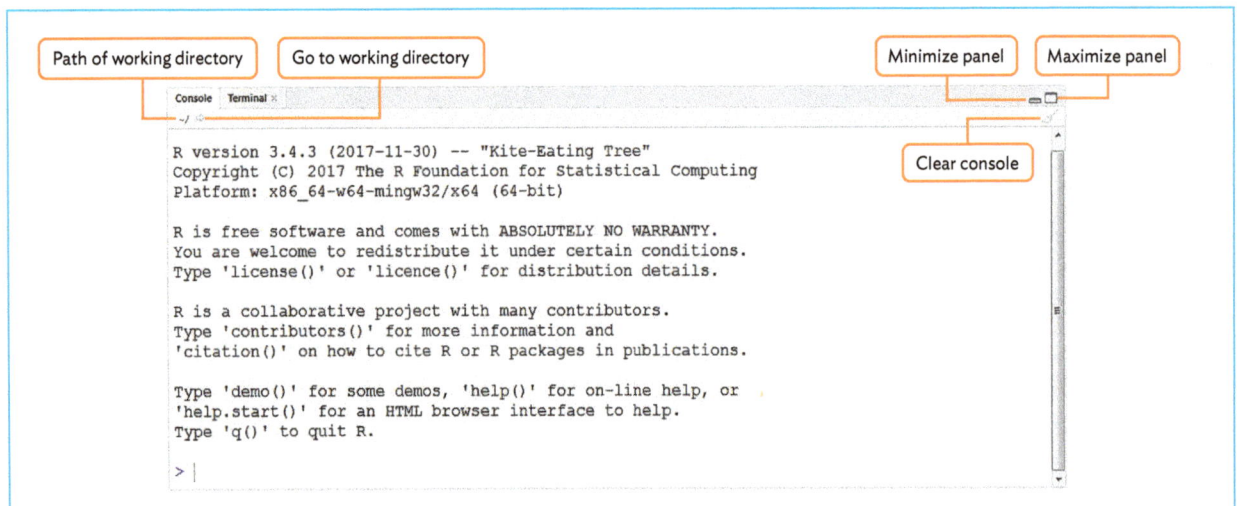

Source: Authors' screenshot of RStudio.

Panel 3 contains tabs for Files, Plots, Packages, and Help (Figure 3.7). The Files tab acts like a file explorer window and displays all files available on the directory.

Figure 3.7: Files Tab in RStudio

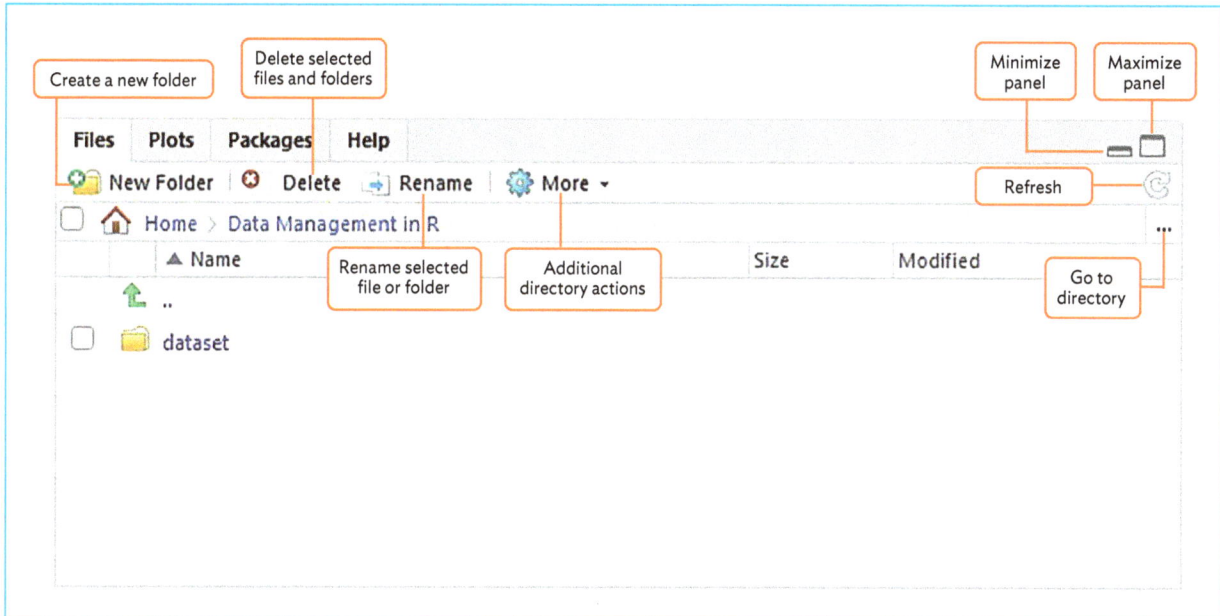

Source: Authors' screenshot of RStudio.

The Plots tab displays the output from running visualizations scripts executed by the user (Figure 3.8).

Figure 3.8: Plots Tab in RStudio

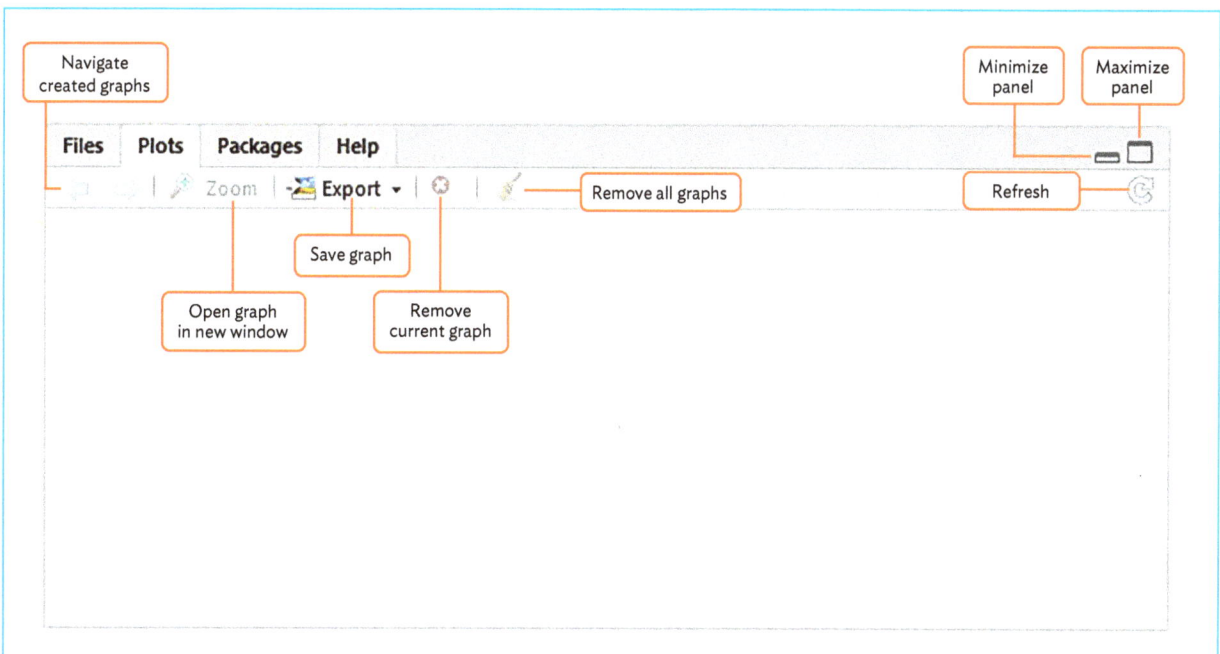

Source: Authors' screenshot of RStudio.

The Packages tab lists all currently installed and loaded packages in RStudio (Figure 3.9).

Figure 3.9: Packages Tab in RStudio

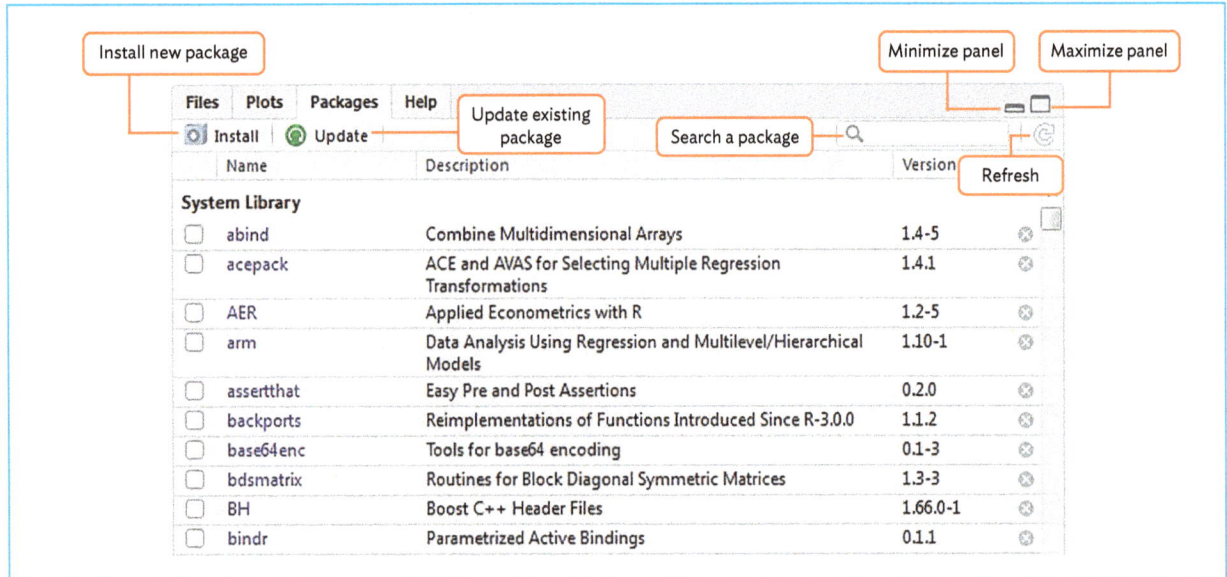

Source: Authors' screenshot of RStudio.

The Help tab provides R and RStudio resources and command documentations (Figure 3.10).

Figure 3.10: Help Tab in RStudio

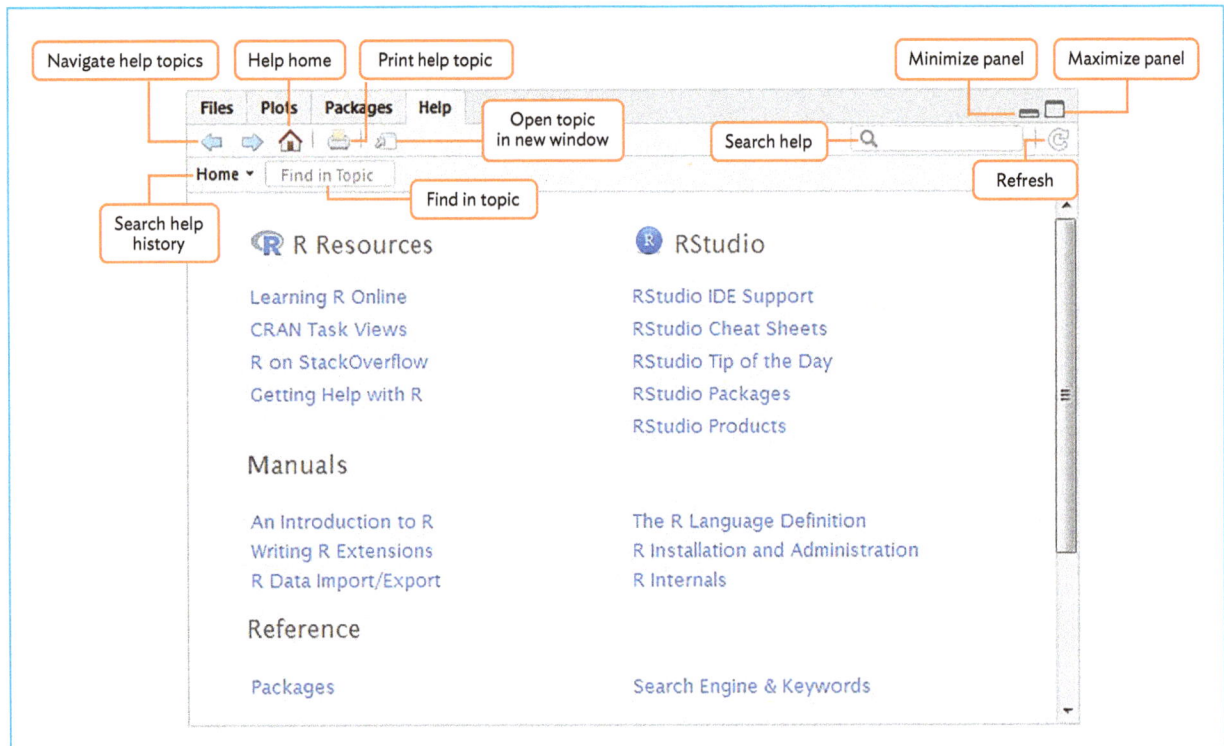

Source: Authors' screenshot of RStudio.

Panel 4 contains tabs for Environment and History. The Environment tab stores and displays any object users create during an RStudio session (Figure 3.11). The History tab keeps a record of all previously executed commands (Figure 3.12).

Figure 3.11: Environment Tab in RStudio

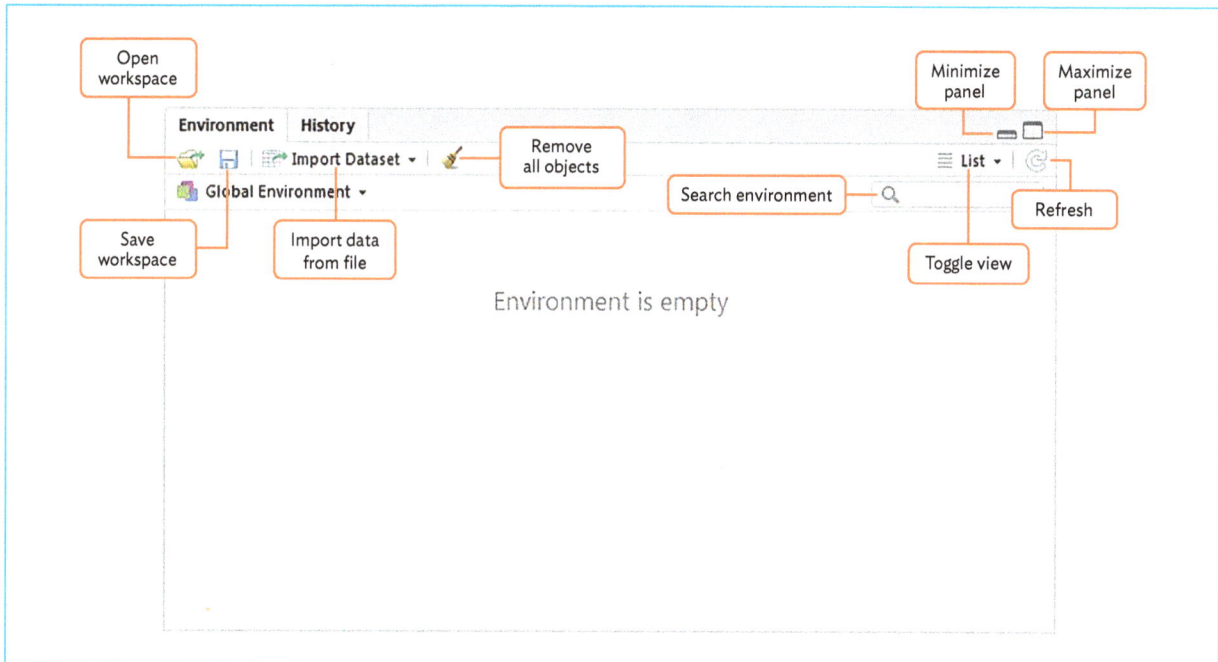

Source: Authors' screenshot of RStudio.

Figure 3.12: History Tab in RStudio

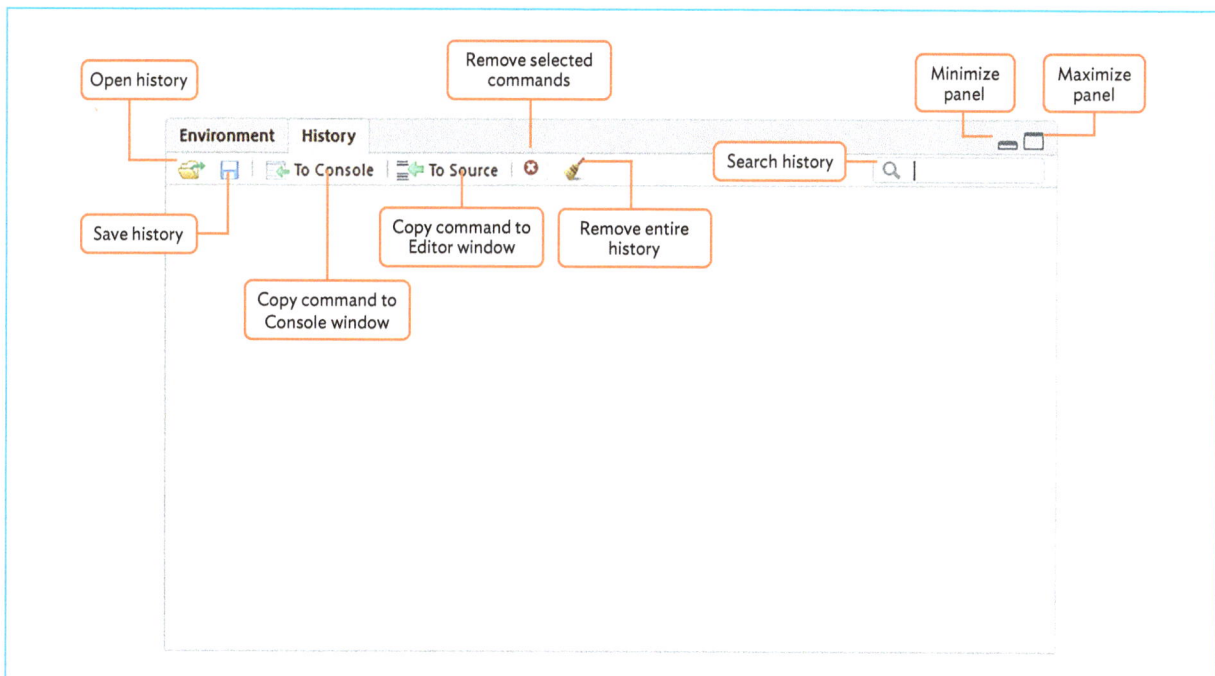

Source: Authors' screenshot of RStudio.

3.1.2   R Packages

Packages are a fundamental feature of R. These collections of R functions, data, compiled code, and documentations are written in a well-defined format that solves problems on a specific domain. Installation of R includes the base package (i.e., the basic functions needed to execute elementary tasks such as simple calculations and importing of text data files). Complex tasks may require intensive coding using base functions, but they are made easier by user-contributed packages.

The Comprehensive R Archive Network (CRAN) currently contains more than 14,000 user-contributed packages, and the number is still growing. Advanced users of R may also install packages from code sharing repositories such as GitHub.

To install a package in RStudio from CRAN, input

install.packages("<name of package>")

Ensure that the computer with RStudio is connected to the internet; otherwise, running the command will throw an error. Verify that the package is installed by checking the Packages tab. Using commands from a package requires loading the package into RStudio, using the command

library(<name of package>)

Alternatively, packages may be installed and loaded in RStudio from the Packages tab by following these steps:

Step 1. Go to the Packages tab and click on Install. An "Install Packages" window will appear (Figure 3.13).

Figure 3.13: Install Packages Window

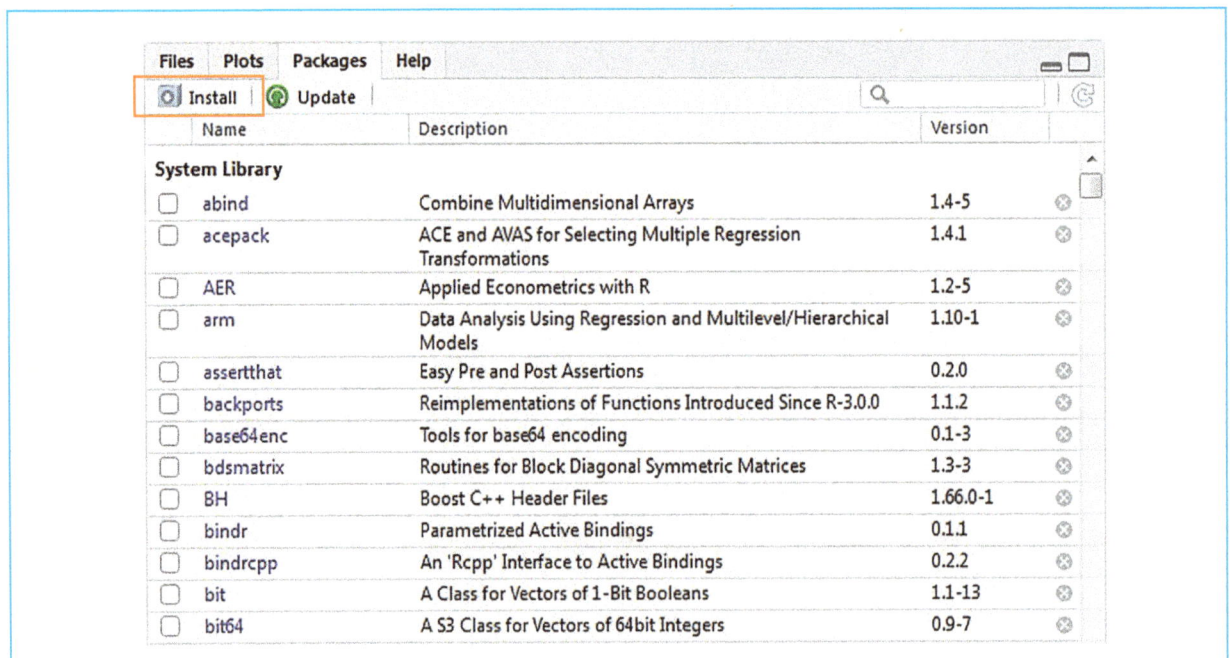

Name	Description	Version
System Library		
abind	Combine Multidimensional Arrays	1.4-5
acepack	ACE and AVAS for Selecting Multiple Regression Transformations	1.4.1
AER	Applied Econometrics with R	1.2-5
arm	Data Analysis Using Regression and Multilevel/Hierarchical Models	1.10-1
assertthat	Easy Pre and Post Assertions	0.2.0
backports	Reimplementations of Functions Introduced Since R-3.0.0	1.1.2
base64enc	Tools for base64 encoding	0.1-3
bdsmatrix	Routines for Block Diagonal Symmetric Matrices	1.3-3
BH	Boost C++ Header Files	1.66.0-1
bindr	Parametrized Active Bindings	0.1.1
bindrcpp	An 'Rcpp' Interface to Active Bindings	0.2.2
bit	A Class for Vectors of 1-Bit Booleans	1.1-13
bit64	A S3 Class for Vectors of 64bit Integers	0.9-7

Source: Authors' screenshot of RStudio.

Step 2. Type the name of the desired package in the Packages input text box and select the appropriate package. RStudio has an autocomplete feature that lists all packages that match the user's string input. To install multiple packages, separate the names with a space or a comma (Figure 3.14). Note that package names are case-sensitive. Once all packages are listed, click on Install.

Figure 3.14: Installing Multiple Packages in RStudio

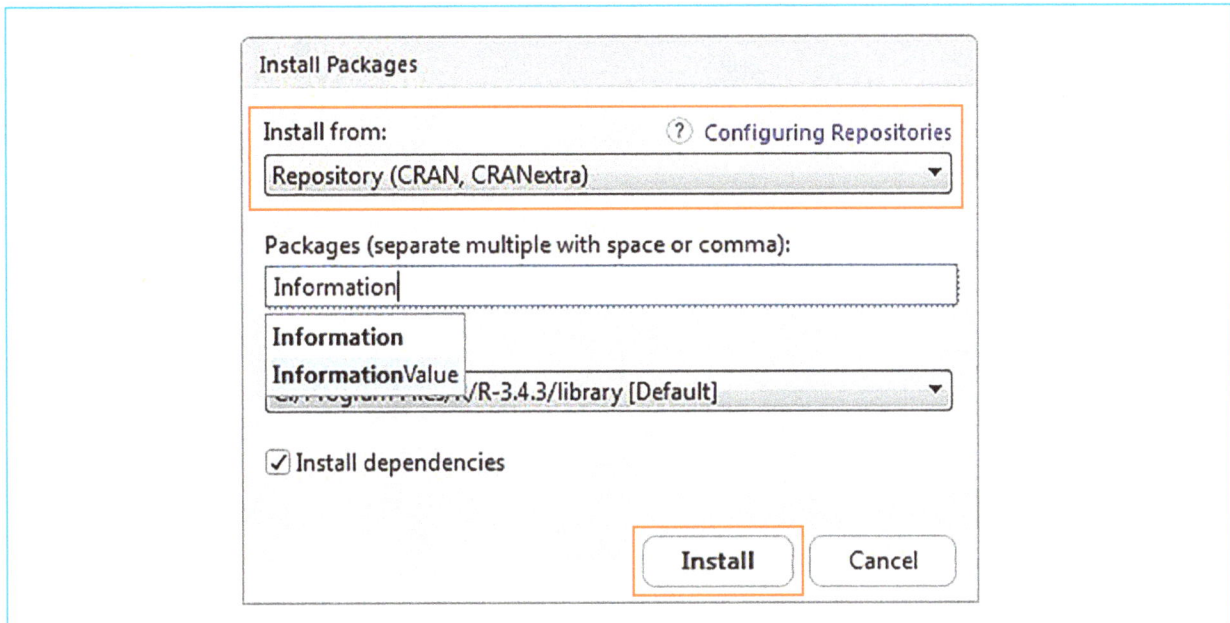

Source: Authors' screenshot of RStudio.

Step 3. Verify installation of the package in RStudio by scrolling through the list of packages or by using the search bar (Figure 3.15).

Figure 3.15: List of Packages in RStudio

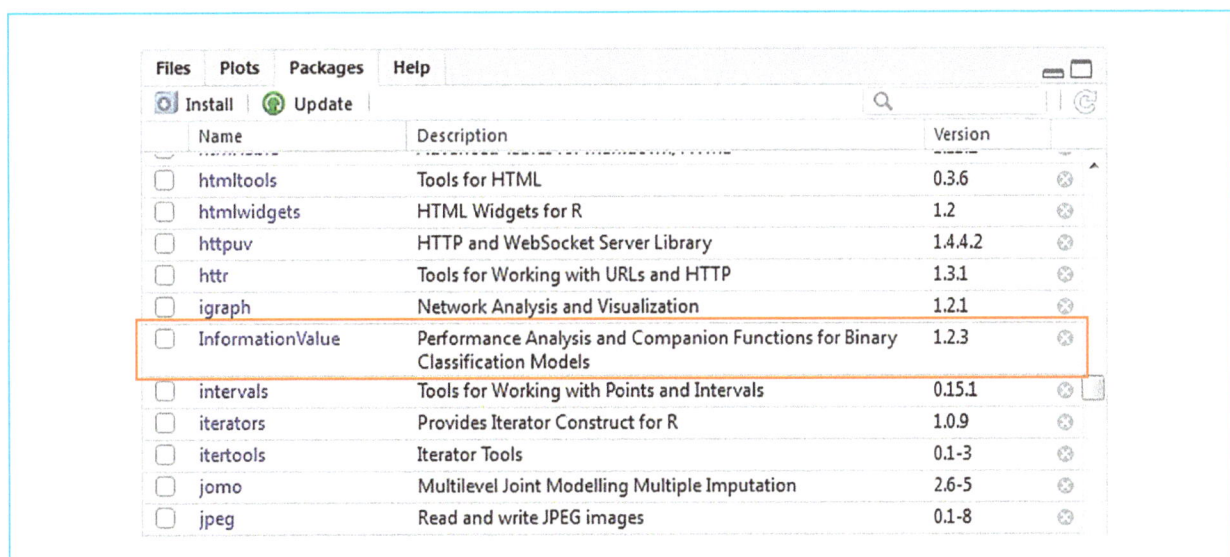

Source: Authors' screenshot of RStudio.

Step 4. To load the package in RStudio, tick the checkbox next to the name of the package (Figure 3.16).

Figure 3.16: Loading the Package in RStudio

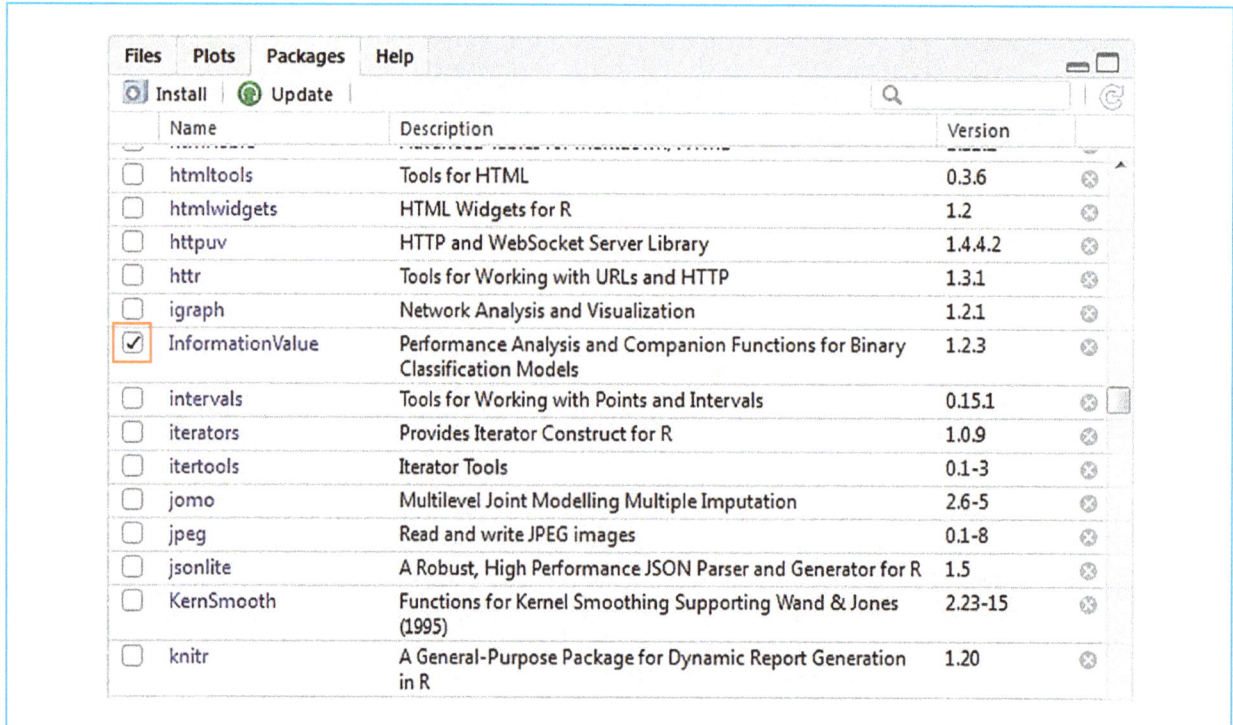

	Name	Description	Version	
☐	htmltools	Tools for HTML	0.3.6	⊗
☐	htmlwidgets	HTML Widgets for R	1.2	⊗
☐	httpuv	HTTP and WebSocket Server Library	1.4.4.2	⊗
☐	httr	Tools for Working with URLs and HTTP	1.3.1	⊗
☐	igraph	Network Analysis and Visualization	1.2.1	⊗
☑	InformationValue	Performance Analysis and Companion Functions for Binary Classification Models	1.2.3	⊗
☐	intervals	Tools for Working with Points and Intervals	0.15.1	⊗
☐	iterators	Provides Iterator Construct for R	1.0.9	⊗
☐	itertools	Iterator Tools	0.1-3	⊗
☐	jomo	Multilevel Joint Modelling Multiple Imputation	2.6-5	⊗
☐	jpeg	Read and write JPEG images	0.1-8	⊗
☐	jsonlite	A Robust, High Performance JSON Parser and Generator for R	1.5	⊗
☐	KernSmooth	Functions for Kernel Smoothing Supporting Wand & Jones (1995)	2.23-15	⊗
☐	knitr	A General-Purpose Package for Dynamic Report Generation in R	1.20	⊗

Source: Authors' screenshot of RStudio.

Some commands used to implement SAE are from packages that do not come pre-installed in RStudio. Therefore, it is necessary to install and load these packages before executing the SAE implementation codes discussed later in the module.

3.1.3 Getting Help and Documentation

It is common to encounter error messages when doing analysis in RStudio and troubleshooting such messages can be a time-consuming task. Many free resources and documentations are available in RStudio and online to help users fix their issues. The Help tab in RStudio, which offers extensive documentation for any command-related issues, can be accessed in different ways, including

- going to the Help tab, typing the command name in the search bar, and pressing Enter on the keyboard (Figure 3.17).

- running the **help()** command with the command name as the parameter, or running the ? operator followed by the name of the command in the Editor or Console window (Figure 3.18). The documentation will be displayed on the Help tab. For example,

  help(optimalCutoff) or ?optimalCutoff

Figure 3.17: Accessing Help Tab in RStudio

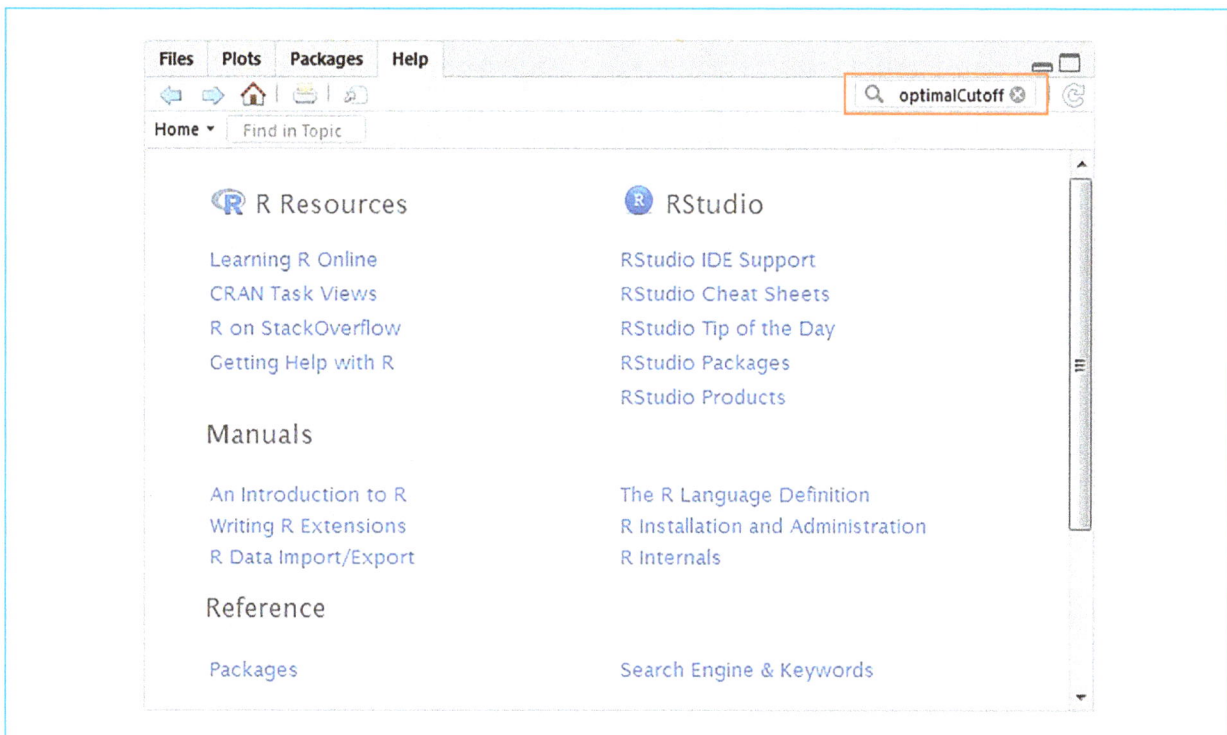

Source: Authors' screenshot of RStudio.

Figure 3.18: Running Help Command in RStudio

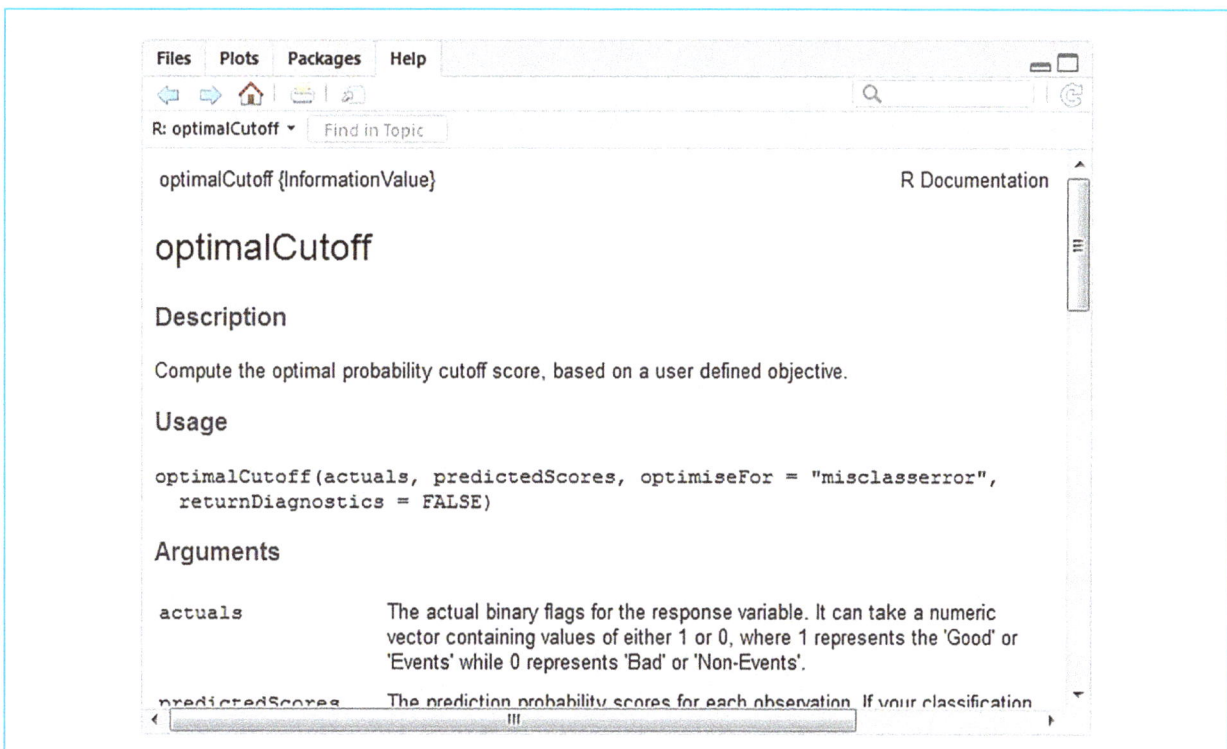

Source: Authors' screenshot of RStudio.

3.2 Fundamentals of R

3.2.1 Arithmetic, Logical, and Relational Operators

In its simplest form, R can act as a calculator and perform basic arithmetic (Table 3.1).

Table 3.1. Basic Arithmetic Operators in R

Operators	Description
+	Addition
-	Subtraction
*	Multiplication
/	Division
^ or **	Exponentiation
%%	Modulus (Remainder from Division)
%/%	Integer Division

Source: RStudio.

Aside from arithmetic operations, R can also evaluate logical and relational statements (Table 3.2).

Table 3.2. Logical and Relational Operators in R

Operators	Description
<, <=	Less than, Less than or equal to
>, >=	Greater than, Greater than or equal to
==	Equality
!=	Non-equality
&	Logical and
|	Logical or

Source: RStudio.

3.2.2 Basic Data Types

A strong understanding of R requires a solid grasp of its basic data types. R has five basic data types, including

- Boolean (**TRUE, FALSE, T, F**)
- Character (**"A", "B", "C", "Poverty", "employed"**)
- Integer (**1L, 2L, 42L, 360L**)
- Numeric (**1, 2.1, 3.14, 525.6**)
- Complex (**1+i, 2–4i, -2i, -7+3i**)

3.2.3 Basic Data Structures

Data structures are the objects that are manipulated inside RStudio. R has four basic data structures: (i) vector, (ii) matrix, (iii) data frame, and (iv) list. The most basic data structure is the vector, which is a one-dimensional object containing elements of the same data type. The matrix is a two-dimensional object, where elements of the same data type are arranged in rows and columns. The data frame is a collection of same-length vectors, whose elements are arranged in rows and columns. Unlike matrices, data frames can include different data types in each column. Most data sets take the form of data frames, because rows may represent observations and columns may represent characteristics of the observations. Finally, lists are collections of objects. Because the elements of a list can be vectors, matrices, data frames, or another list, it is among the most complex and flexible data structures.

3.2.4 Setting the Working Directory

The working directory (i.e., the active computer folder) is the location where RStudio will look when accessing files. Therefore, it is important to set the working directory before starting an analysis. To check the current working directory of the RStudio session, type the command

```
getwd()
```

To set the working directory to another location, type the command

```
setwd("<folder path>")
```

This command assigns the folder as the new working directory of the current RStudio session. Every time a new RStudio session is started, the working directory is set to the default location, and users may need to change the working directory to the folder where they will access their working files.

Alternatively, the users can set the working directory in the Files tab by following these steps:

Step 1. Navigate to the folder that will be set as the working directory (Figure 3.19).

Figure 3.19: Navigating the Folder for Setting the Working Directory

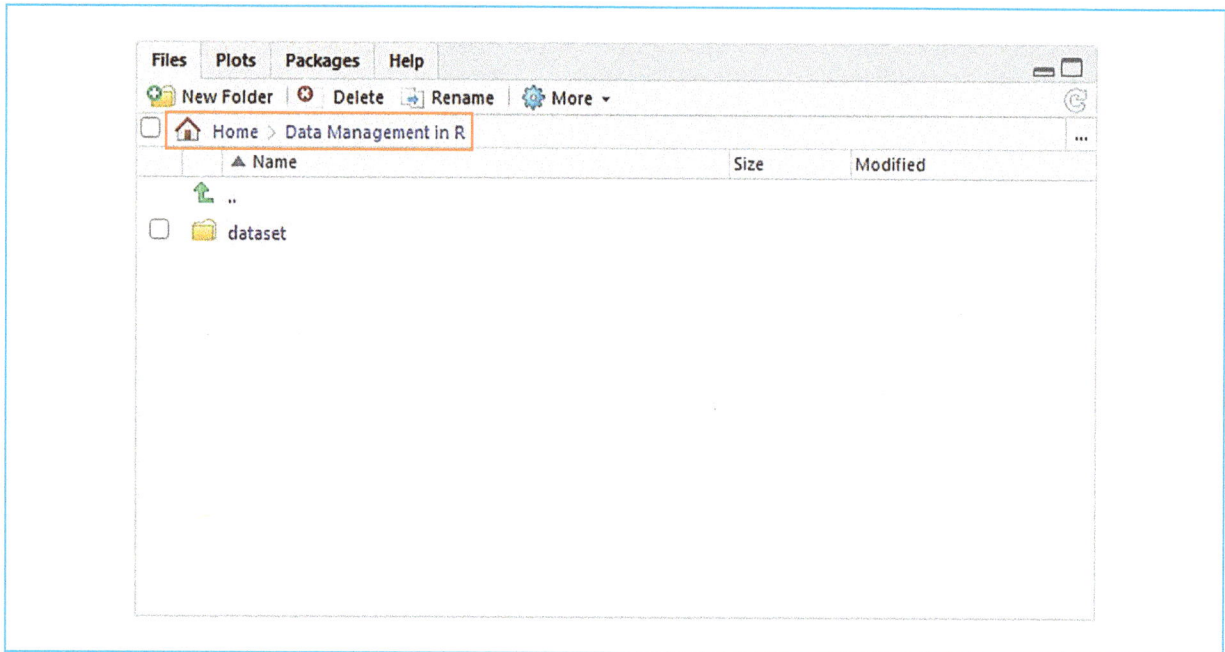

Source: Authors' screenshot of RStudio.

Step 2. Click on More > Set As Working Directory (Figure 3.20).

Figure 3.20: Setting the Working Directory

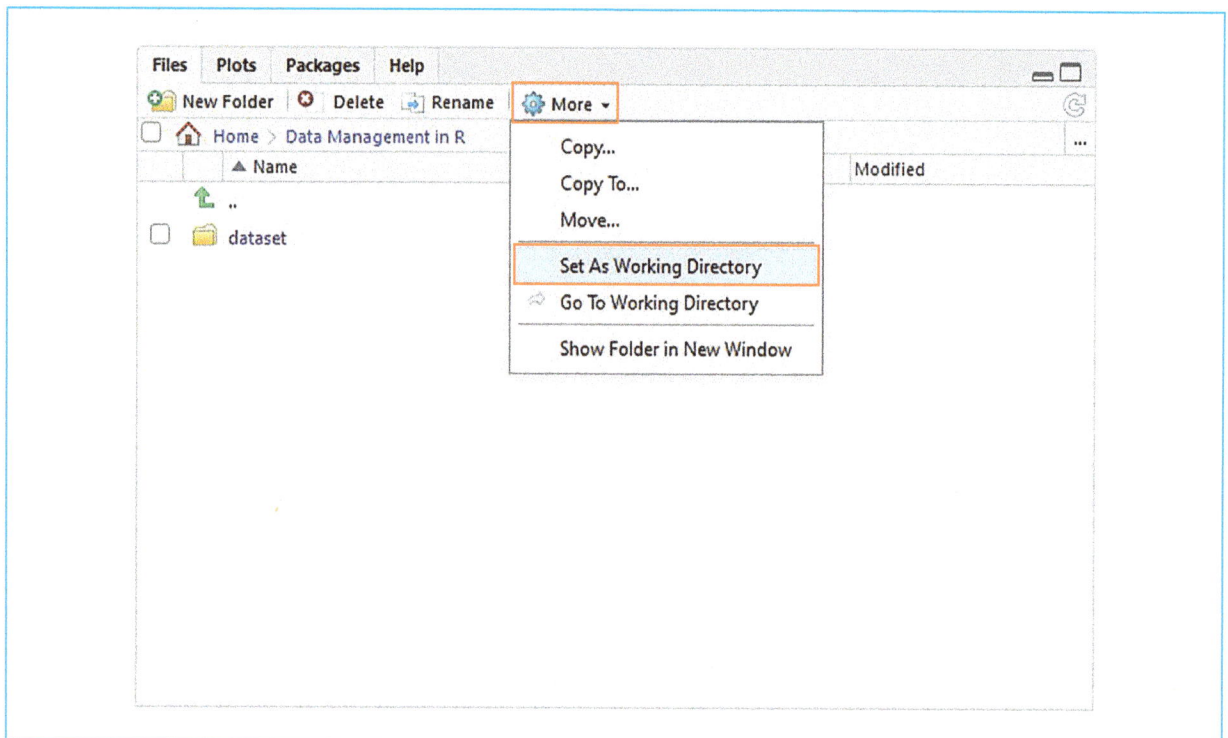

Source: Authors' screenshot of RStudio.

3.2.5 Importing and Exporting Data Sets

After setting the working directory, users can import data files from the working directory to RStudio. Importing simple text files in RStudio is easy. Assign a file name using one of the following base commands:

> <name of data frame> <- read.table("<text filename>")
>
> **or**
>
> <name of data frame> <- read.csv("<text filename>")

Additional parameters can be set to modify how RStudio interprets the input data. The text files are imported in RStudio as objects that can be manipulated to suit the needs of the analysis. To view the imported data sets, use the command

> View(<name of data frame>)

To export a data frame from RStudio into a text or csv file, use the command

> write.table(<name of data frame>, "<filename>")

where the first argument is the object containing the data and the filename is the name of the text or csv file as it appears in the working directory. This command must include the filename extension.

If the relevant packages have been installed and loaded, data files from other applications can be imported and exported to and from RStudio. Table 3.3 shows some examples.

Table 3.3. R Packages for Importing and Exporting Data Files from Different Applications

Application	Package	Command	Task
Excel	readxl	read_excel()	Import
	writexl	write_xlsx()	Export
SAS	foreign	read.xport()	Import
		write.foreign()	Export
SPSS		read.spss()	Import
		write.foreign()	Export
Stata		read.dta()	Import
		write.dta()	Export

SAS= Statistical Analysis Software, SPSS =Statistical Package for the Social Sciences.
Source: RStudio.

Aside from manually typing import commands in the Editor or Console window, users may also use the Import Data Set tool (in the Environment tab) to load data sets in RStudio. The tool provides an interface where users can select their data file from a browser, preview the data, and specify import options. Access the tool by going to the Environment tab, clicking on the Import Data Set button, and selecting the type of file that will be imported (Figure 3.21).

Figure 3.21: Importing Data Sets in Environment Tab

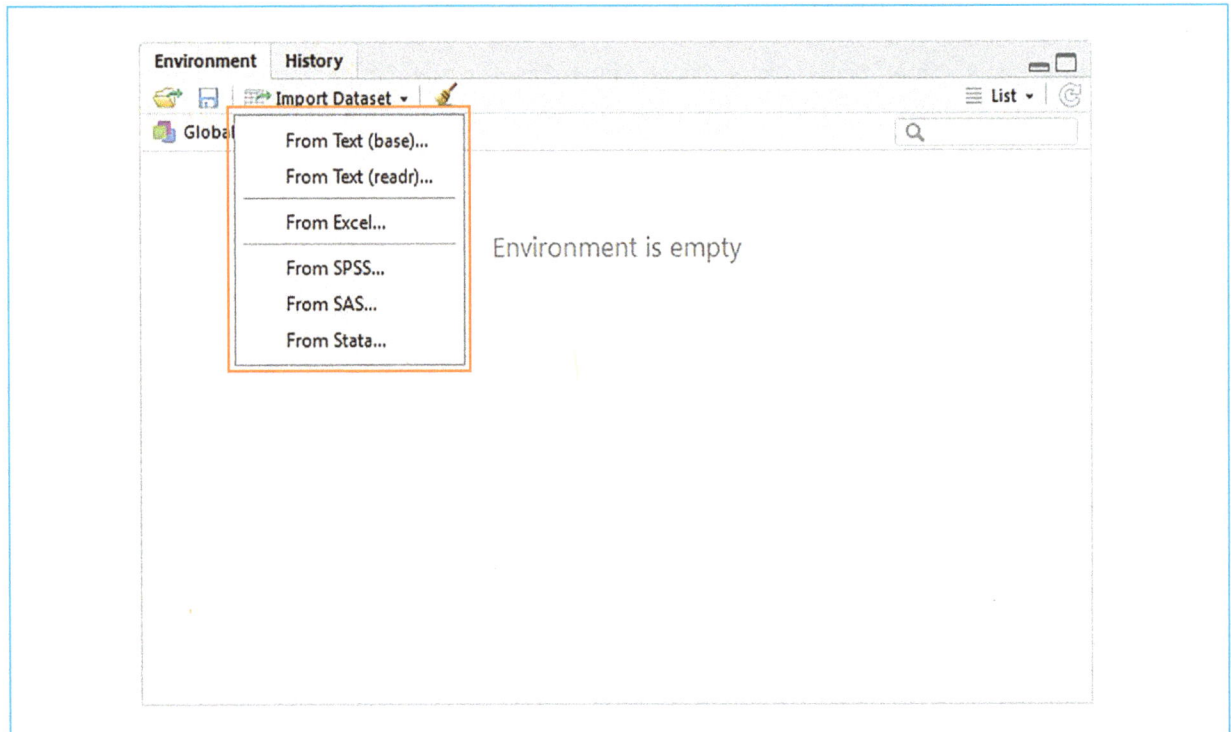

Source: Authors' screenshot of RStudio.

Other packages that import and export RStudio's various data files contain additional features and commands that may be helpful. It is the users' discretion to choose a package that meets their requirements.

3.2.6 Creating and Updating Objects

To assign a name to a value or an object, use the equal sign (**=**) or arrow (**<-**) operator:

<object name> <- <a value, an object or a dataset>

This action assigns the value or object on the right to the object name on the left. Note that if the object name already exists in the current RStudio session, the program will overwrite the contents of that object name. Users must be aware of the following restrictions when naming an object:

- Object names must start with a letter or a period. Names that start with a period cannot be followed by a number.
- Object names can be a combination of letters, numbers, periods, and underscores.
- Object names must not be a reserved word in R.

For example, load the **countryx_demographics_01.xlsx** Excel file and assign it to the name df. This data set contains information on the seven provinces of Country X, including the region code (**r_code**), province name (**province**), female (**f_popn**) and male (**m_popn**) population, and land area (**area**).

```
setwd("~/dataset")
install.packages("readxl")
library(readxl)
df <- read_excel("countryx_demographics_01.xlsx")
```

To delete or remove an object from the current RStudio session, use the command

```
rm(name of object)
```

3.2.7 Creating and Updating Variables

When exploring data, it may be useful to consider new variables derived from existing variables. To create or update a variable (column) in a data frame, specify (i) the name of the data frame, followed by (ii) the **$** operator and (iii) the name of the variable. When using an existing variable name, the values for that variable will be overwritten; creating a new name will add a new variable in the data frame. The values could be hard-coded or based on calculation.

```
<data frame name>$<column name> <- <value or calculation>
```

For example,

➤ Create a total population (**tot_popn**) in **df** by adding the female (**f_popn**) and male (**m_popn**) populations.

```
df$tot_popn <- df$f_popn + df$m_popn
```

➤ In **df**, the land area (**area**) variable is measured in square kilometers. Update its values to display the land area in square meters.

```
df$area <- df$area * 1000000
```

3.2.8 Basic Subsetting

In some cases, users are interested in only a small portion of the data for a particular analysis. R has fast subsetting features to select relevant observations and variables, which can be performed in several ways:

(a) Using [ ] Operator

Through R's powerful indexing feature, users can select columns and filter rows by specifying the position of variables and observations in an object. There are two indexes involved when subsetting a data frame: the first is used to specify the rows to filter, while the second is used to specify the columns to select. Absence of the row index will return all rows, absence of the column index will return all columns, and absence of both will return the original data frame.

```
<data frame name>[<row indices>, <column indices>]
```

Aside from specifying the row index, a more common approach to filtering observations is to use a condition. Only the observations that meet the condition will be included in the final data frame. The **$**, logical and relational operators are used regularly to specify conditions. For example,

- Filter the data frame **df** for the first four observations and the first, third, and fourth columns.

    df[1:4, c(1, 3, 4)]

- Filter the data frame **df** for observations that have 400,000 females or fewer, and return all columns.

    df[df$f_popn <= 400000,]

(b) Using Subset()

The subset command requires two arguments to perform subsetting: the data frame and a condition to filter observations. A third optional argument is the list of columns to be selected. The syntax to run the subset command is

    subset(x = <name of data frame>,
        subset = <condition/s>,
        select = <column/s (optional)>)

For example, use the subset command to filter the data frame **df** for observations that have 400,000 females or fewer, and return the province name (**province**), female (**f_popn**) and male (**m_popn**) populations, and land area (**area**) variables.

    subset(x = df,
        subset = f_popn <= 400000,
        select = c("province", "f_popn", "m_popn", "area"))

3.2.9 Data Inspection

After importing the data into RStudio, users can start to perform basic data exploration. The following commands are used to examine the data set (Table 3.4).

Table 3.4: R Commands for Examining Data Sets

Command	Description
length() dim() ncol() nrow()	Determine the dimensions of an object
names colnames() rownames()	Retrieve the set of row or column names of an object
str()	Displays the internal structure of an object
head() tail()	View the first or last observations of an object
unique()	Returns all possible values of an object
summary()	Displays summary statistics from a data frame
factor()	Encodes an object as a category

Source: RStudio.

■ Calculate basic statistics from a variable in a data frame, using the following commands (Table 3.5).

Table 3.5: R Commands for Basic Statistics

Command	Description
sum()	Calculates the sum
mean()	Calculates the average
median()	Calculates the median
min()	Returns the minimum
max()	Returns the maximum
sd()	Calculates the standard deviation
var()	Calculates the variance

Source: RStudio.

For example,

➤ Display the number of observations and variables in the **df** object.

```
dim(df)
```

➤ Display the variable names of **df**.

```
colnames(df)
```

➤ Display the structure of the **df** object.

```
str(df)
```

➤ Extract the first two observations of the **df** object.

```
head(df, 2)
```

➤ Calculate summary statistics for every variable in **df**.

```
summary(df)
```

➤ Encode the region code (r_code) variable in **df** as a category.

```
df$r_code <- factor(df$r_code)
```

➤ Compute the total land area of Country X.

```
sum(df$area)
```

3.2.10   Merging Data Sets

Combining data from different sources is common in data analysis, because it provides more information about your data set. Merging data set in R can be done in several ways, including combining data set row-wise using **rbind()** and column-wise using **cbind()**.

The simplest merge is when two data frames have identical columns or an identical number of rows. The rbind command is used to append a data frame to another data frame as new rows, while the cbind command is used to append a data frame to another data frame as new columns. To use the rbind and cbind commands,

```
rbind(<data frame 1>, <data frame 2>)
cbind(<data frame 1>, <data frame 2>)
```

When using these commands remember that

- the rbind command requires users to ensure that the two data frames are identical in the number of columns, column names, and data type per column; and
- the cbind command requires users to ensure that the data frames have the same number of rows and that the order at which the observations appear in each data frame is the same (i.e., the first row in the first data frame and the first row in the second data frame are the same observation).

For example,

> import the **country_demographics_02.xlsx** to load the information on the remaining provinces of Country X. Use the rbind command to append this data set row-wise to the **df** object and assign the combined data frame to the **demographics** object. Verify that the resulting data frame contains the combined information.

```
df_02 <- read_excel("countryx_demographics_02.xlsx")
demographics <- rbind(df, df_02)
View(demographics)
```

> import the **countryx_home.xlsx** file which contains the number of homes for all provinces in Country X. Update the **demographics** data frame by using cbind to append the home data column-wise. Verify that the resulting data frame has been updated with the new information.

```
home <- read_excel("countryx_home.xlsx")
demographics <- cbind(demographics, home)
View(demographics)
```

> Combine data set using **merge()**.

The merge command is used to combine data when it isn't as straightforward as simply appending rows or columns. When the merge command is used on two data frames, they are combined using a key, which is a variable (or set of variables) that uniquely identifies an observation. In simple cases, one variable is sufficient to identify an observation. In other cases, multiple variables may be needed. This key must be present in both data frames because it is used to match observations from one data frame to the other. The resulting merged data frame contains all columns from the two data frames. Which observations are included in the resulting data frame will depend on the type of merge. To merge two data frames in RStudio, type the command

```
merge(x = <data frame 1>, y = <data frame 2>,
      by = <key>, all/all.x/all.y = <TRUE/FALSE>)
```

where **x** and **y** are the data frame to be combined, **by** is the column or set of columns containing the key, and **all**, **all.x** and **all.y** are merge criteria arguments. Strictly one merge criteria argument is needed in the merge command. To include all observations from the two data frames in the resulting data frame, the **all** argument should be used and must be set to **TRUE (all = TRUE)**. If **all** is set to **FALSE (all = FALSE)**, only the common observations from the two data frames are included in the resulting data frame. To include all observations from the first data frame and only the common observations from the second data, use the **all.x** argument, set to **TRUE (all.x = TRUE)**. To include all observations from the second data frame and only the common observations from the first data frame, the **all.y** argument should be used and set to **TRUE (all.y = TRUE)**.

For example, import the **countryx_poverty_rate.xlsx** and assign it to the **pov_rate** object. This data set contains poverty rate on select provinces of Country X. Merge this data frame to the **demographics** object such that all observations from both data frames are retained. Assign the resulting data frame to the **demog_and_pov object**.

```
pov_rate <- read_excel("countryx_poverty_rate.xlsx")
demog_and_pov <- merge(x = demographics,
           y = pov_rate,
           by = "province",
           all = TRUE)
```

3.3 Data Manipulation Using dplyr and tidyr

Data sets come in different forms and sizes, and often require rigorous manipulation to organize them into a format that is easy to work with. In 2019, Wickham developed an R package suite called **tidyverse** (CRAN 2019), which contains tools that share an underlying design philosophy, grammar, and data structure. To install and load the individual packages in RStudio, type the following command

```
install.packages(c("dplyr", "tidyr"))
library(dplyr)
library(tidyr)
```

3.3.1 The dplyr Package

This R package is a grammar of data manipulation, providing a consistent set of commands that help solve the most common data manipulation challenges. The dplyr package has seven fundamental commands:

3.3.1.1 Select columns with select()

Large data sets can be troublesome, especially if RStudio is running on limited computer memory. The "select" command allows the extraction and/or removal of columns from the data set so that users are left only with columns that are of interest to them. The syntax for the select command is

```
select(<data frame>, <column/s to select>)
```

3.3.1.2 Filter observations with filter()

While the select command operates on the columns of the data set, the filter command operates on the rows and subsets observations based on condition/s. Logical and relational operators are commonly used to specify these conditions. The syntax for the filter command is

filter(<data frame>, <condition/s>)

3.3.1.3 Create new variables with mutate()

The $ operator is one method to create new variables in the data set. The dplyr package has the mutate command, which serves a similar purpose. The syntax for the mutate command is

mutate(<data frame>, <new variable> = <formula>)

3.3.1.4 Sort observations with arrange()

Arrange the observations in ascending or descending order using the arrange command. By default, the arrange command sorts the data in ascending order. To sort the data in descending order, use the desc(<sorting variable>) command inside arrange. The syntax for the arrange command is

arrange(<data frame>, <sorting variable/s>)

3.3.1.5 Rename Columns with rename()

Change the column names of the data set using the rename command. The syntax for the rename command is

rename(<data frame>, <new column name> = <old column name>)

3.3.1.6 Change the Unit of Analysis with group_by()

The "group_by" command updates the unit of analysis when users wish to perform calculations by group. All fundamental commands of dplyr and tidyr can be used in conjunction with the group_by command. The syntax for the group_by command is

group_by(<data frame>, <grouping variable/s>)

3.3.1.7 Calculate Aggregate Summaries with summarise()

The summarise command provides grouped summary for the data set. By default, this command treats the data set as one big group and provides summary statistics of the entire data set. It is best used with the group_by command to change the unit of analysis from the complete data set to individual groups. The syntax for the summarise command is

summarise(group_by(<data frame>),
    <formula for summary statistic>)

For example, using the **demog_and_pov** data set,

> select region code, province, and female population variables
>
> select(demog_and_pov, r_code, province, f_popn)

> filter observations with less than 500,000 men and poverty rate = 10% or higher
>
> filter(demog_and_pov, m_popn < 500000, pov_rate > 10)

> create a total population variable by adding female and male population
>
> mutate(demog_and_pov, tot_popn = f_popn + m_popn)

> sort the data set in ascending order of poverty rate
>
> arrange(demog_and_pov, pov_rate)

> rename the female population variable (f_popn) to female_popn and the male population to male_popn
>
> rename(demog_and_pov, female_popn = f_popn,
>   male_popn = m_popn)

> group the data by region code and compute the total female and total male population per region
>
> summarise(group_by(demog_and_pov, r_code),
>   tot_f_popn = sum(f_popn),
>   tot_m_popn = sum(m_popn))

3.3.2   The tidyr Package

Tidyr provides a set of functions that help transform data sets into tidy data. Wickham defines tidy data as data with a consistent form, where every variable is in a column (Wickham 2013). There are two fundamental commands in the tidyr package:

- Transform data set from wide to long format with **gather()**.

  A common problem in data sets is where column names are not names of variables, but values of a variable. The gather command collapses multiple columns into two columns: key and value. The key column will contain the former column names while the value column will contain the values for each cell. The syntax for the gather command is

      gather(<data frame>, <key column name>, <value column name>,
             <columns to collapse>)

- Transform data set from long to wide format with **spread()**.

  The spread command is used to create new columns from unique values of a variable. This command is the opposite of gather. The syntax for the spread command is

```
spread(<data frame>, <column name of key>,
        <column name of value>)
```

For example,

➤ Import the **wide_poverty.xlsx** file and assign it to the **reg_pov_rate** object. This data set contains the regional poverty rate of Country X from 2014 to 2016. Use the gather command to create a year variable **(year)** and a poverty rate variable **(pov_rate)** containing the corresponding poverty rate for that year.

```
reg_pov_rate <- read_excel("wide_poverty.xlsx")
gather(reg_pov_rate, "year", "pov_rate", 2:4)
```

➤ Import the **long_population.xlsx** file and assign it to the **reg_popn** object. This data set contains the regional population count by sex of Country X. Use the spread command to create male and female variables containing their corresponding population values.

```
reg_popn <- read_excel("long_population.xlsx")
spread(reg_popn, "sex", "population")
```

3.3.3 The Pipe Operator

Exploring a data set entails a lot of data manipulation (e.g., creating new variables and calculating aggregated summaries), which may lead to chaining the sequence of commands from the dplyr and tidyr packages. From a readability and coding standpoint, this could be a bit overwhelming and could slow down the coding process since each step requires construction of an intermediate data frame to be used in the next step in the sequence of commands. Piping addresses this issue. The pipe operator—denoted by %>%—takes the object on its left hand side and treats it as the first parameter of the command on its right hand side. The piping command makes the code more readable and easier to understand. To use the pipe operator,

```
<object> %>%
    <command 1> %>%
    <command 2>
```

For example,

➤ Filter the **demog_and_pov** data for provinces that have more than 500,000 men. Return the region code (**r_code**), province name (**province**) and male population (**m_popn**).

```
demog_and_pov %>%
    select(r_code, province, m_popn) %>%
    filter(m_popn > 500000)
```

➤ Filter the **demog_and_pov** data for province with poverty rate higher than 5%. Calculate the total population and population density for those provinces and return the province name (**province**), total population (**tot_popn**) and population density (**pop_dens**) only.

```
demog_and_pov %>%
    filter(pov_rate > 5) %>%
    mutate(tot_popn = f_popn + m_popn,
        pop_dens = tot_popn / area) %>%
    select(province, tot_popn, pop_dens)
```

➤ Calculate the total female (**tot_f_popn**) and total male (**tot_m_popn**) population per region from the **demog_and_pov** data.

```
demog_and_pov %>%
    group_by(r_code) %>%
    summarise(tot_f_popn = sum(f_popn),
        tot_m_popn = sum(m_popn))
```

3.4 Linear Regression in R

Linear regression is a very simple tool for predicting a quantitative response (i.e., dependent variable) based on one or more predictor variables (i.e., independent variables). It assumes that there is an approximately linear relationship between the dependent and independent variables, which generates an equation that describes the relationship. Mathematically, this is written as

$$Y = \beta_0 + \beta_1 X_1 + \beta_2 X_2 + \cdots + \beta_k X_k + \varepsilon,$$

where Y is the dependent variable, $X_1 \ldots X_k$ are the independent variables, β_0 is the intercept of the model, $\beta_1 \ldots \beta_k$ are the regression coefficients of the model, and ε is the error term. The intercept of the model can be interpreted as the predicted value of the dependent variable when the independent variable is 0, while the slope of the model is interpreted as the change in the dependent variable for one unit change in the independent variable while holding other factors constant.

3.4.1 Implementation in R

R provides comprehensive support for linear regression, and the glm command can be used to fit generalized linear models. The syntax for the glm command is

```
glm(<formula>, <family>, <data>)
```

where the formula is of the form **y ~ x₁ + x₂ + x₃**, which is a symbolic expression of the model to be fitted, with **y** representing the dependent variable and **xᵢ**'s representing the independent variables, family is a description of the error distribution and link function to be used in the model, and data is the data frame containing the variables in the model.

Linear models can be stored in an object by using an assignment operator. The summary statistics of the model can be printed by running the command

```
summary(<model object name>)
```

The output of the command displays summary statistics of the residuals, the coefficient table with the corresponding standard errors and significance values, and some model assessment measures.

For example, import the household survey data set from the **hh_survey.xlsx** file and assign it to the object **hh_survey**. Create a simple linear model for expenditure per capita **(tot_exp_per_capita)** using household size **(hhsize)** as the independent variable. Display the summary statistics of the model generated:

```
hh_survey <- read_excel("hh_survey.xlsx")
model <- glm(formula = tot_exp_per_capita ~ hhsize,
        family = gaussian(),
        data = hh_survey)
summary(model)
```

To access individual components of the model summary, use **$**. To check which components are available to extract, use the attributes command

```
attributes(<model object name>)
```

In a good regression model, the results in predicted values are close to the actual values of the dependent variable. Fitted values and residuals can assess the goodness of fit of a regression model. Note that more sophisticated tests and statistics are available in other packages.

3.4.2   Fitted Values and Residuals

The difference between the actual values of the dependent variable versus the predicted values is called the residual. Every observation from the data set has its own residual. To display the predicted values, use the command

```
fitted(<model object name>) or <model object name>$fitted.values
```

To display the residuals, use the command

```
residuals(<model object name>) or <model object name>$residuals
```

3.4.3   Coefficients and p-values

The regression coefficients represent the change in the dependent variable for one unit change in the dependent variable while holding other predictors constant. To display the coefficients of the model, use the command

```
coefficients(<model object name>)
```

or

```
<model object name>$coefficients
```

The p-value tests the null hypothesis that the coefficient has no effect in the model. A low p-value indicates that the null hypothesis can be rejected and that the independent variable is a good addition to the model. On the other hand, a high p-value suggests that the change in the independent variable is not associated with the change in the dependent variable. To display the p-value of the independent variables, use the **$** command

    summary(model)$coefficients

3.5 R Packages for Small Area Estimation

Apart from being a free and easily accessible tool, R is very appealing due to its wide array of packages available at the user's disposal. The commands used to implement SAE come from different packages that were developed by practitioners who once worked on a similar problem (see Chapter IV).

3.5.1 The car Package

This package provides many functions that are applied to a fitted regression model, perform additional calculations in the model or possibly compute a different model, and then return values and graphs.

3.5.2 The sae Package

This package obtains model-based estimates for small areas based on a variety of models at the area and unit levels, along with basic direct and indirect estimates. Mean squared errors are estimated by analytical approximations in simple models and applying bootstrap procedures in more complex models.

3.5.3 The InformationValue Package

This package provides functions for assessing the performance of classification models and optimizing probability cut-off score based on user-specified objectives to aid in accuracy improvement in binary classification models.

3.5.4 The rsq Package

This package calculates generalized R-squared, partial R-squared, and partial correlation coefficients for generalized linear models, including quasi-models with well-defined variance functions.

CHAPTER IV | APPROACHES IN SMALL AREA ESTIMATION

Chapter II briefly discussed key considerations when developing an SAE plan. Many of these considerations have implications on the choice of small area estimation methodology. Although the choice of methodology is crucial, it depends largely on the context such as what is the variable of interest, levels of desired disaggregation, and availability of data.

This chapter enumerates various small area estimation techniques and presents some worked examples on how to implement the methodology using R software. The chapter also outlines the performance of each technique and discusses their advantages and disadvantages.

4.1 Direct Survey Estimation

Suppose a survey's target population can be divided into M domains (D_1, D_2,...D_k,... D_M). Recall that the survey's domain specifies the level at which one can expect to get precise and accurate estimates. This is true because the acceptable levels of precision and accuracy are specified when calculating sample size at the domain level.

If we want to estimate population size (e.g., the total number of poor people), the corresponding direct survey estimator, $\hat{Y}$, is simply the weighted sum of y_j associated with each sampled unit such that

$$\hat{Y} = \sum_{j \in S} w_j y_j ,\qquad (4.1)$$

where y_j is the characteristic of interest (e.g., 1 if the sampled unit is classified as poor, 0 otherwise); and w_j is the sampling weight attached to the jth sampled unit.

Now, suppose we want to estimate $\hat{Y}$ for each of N sub-domains (SD_1, SD_2,..., SD_l,...SD_N). In direct survey estimation, we estimate $\hat{Y}_l$ such that

$$\hat{Y}_l = \sum_{j \in S, j \in SD_l} w_j y_j .\qquad (4.2)$$

Thus, the second equation is a direct analogue of the first, where we only restrict the summation to all sampled units belonging to sub-domain SD_l.

Most direct survey estimators are unbiased because the expected value of the survey is designed such that the estimator approaches the true value of the parameter of interest, on average.

On the other hand, the reliability of a direct survey estimator depends, among other things, on the number of observations used in calculation. If SD_l is significantly smaller than any of the survey domain D_M's, the sampling error of $\hat{Y}_l$ may be higher than ideal.

Hence, although direct survey estimation may be the most straightforward methodology for disaggregating an indicator that is compiled using survey data, its reliability depends on how representative the sampled data collected from SD_i are. If we have too few sampled units from SD_i, SD_i may be considered as a small area.

In direct survey estimation, estimates for small areas should be used with caution. A common practice is to flag estimates with coefficients of variation exceeding a certain level (e.g., 15%). Others avoid publishing estimates that do not meet a certain threshold of reliability level.

As mentioned previously, most currently available software programs provide an algorithm for computing the direct survey estimator and its measure of variability or standard error. A call for the function to compute it using the software is what is needed to get the estimates and corresponding measure of precision.

To illustrate how direct survey estimation can be implemented using R, consider the following example. Suppose we want to estimate poverty rate and its corresponding measure of reliability (i.e., the coefficient of variation) at the national and provincial level. First, we need to install the necessary packages, using the command "install". In R software, the required packages are ***readxl*** and ***survey***.

```
install.packages(c("readxl","survey"), dependencies = TRUE)
library (readxl)
library (survey)
```

The data set for the estimation can be set up with the following command:

```
hies <-read_excel("hies.xlsx")
```

The survey design parameters can be assigned using the command

```
fsvy<-svydesign(ids=~psu, strata=~stratum, weights=~weight, data=hies)
```

Given the data set, direct estimates and corresponding CV for the national and provincial estimates can be obtained using the commands

```
svymean(~poor, fsvy)
cv(svymean(~poor,fsvy))
svyby(~poor, ~regn, fsvy, svymean, vartype=c("cv"), level=0.95)
```

4.2 Small Area Estimation Using Auxiliary Information

The main principle of SAE is to borrow "strength", or, more specifically, provide a more reliable alternative from other data sources to the direct survey estimator. In SAE jargon, these data sources must provide useful "auxiliary information" that can be used to enhance the precision of direct survey estimates.

Auxiliary data may come in different forms. To determine whether a specific type of data provides auxiliary information that can be used to apply a SAE technique, we need to ask the following questions:

- Does the information from data not prone to the "small sample size" problem (e.g., census or administrative data)?
- Is this information correlated with the indicator of interest?
- At what level is the information available?
- Is it available at the same, lower, or higher level as the desired level of disaggregation?

Positive response to the first two questions indicates that SAE is feasible. On the other hand, the response to the last question is key to choosing which SAE technique can be used. The following section discusses general principles of various small area estimation techniques, based on the type of auxiliary data available.

Compared to direct survey estimates, SAE techniques yield estimators that are not necessarily unbiased regarding the survey's sampling design. Thus, proper assessment of small area estimators requires users to examine its mean square error.[9] Nevertheless, while SAE may introduce bias in the calculation, many SAE techniques are designed to produce estimates with acceptable levels of accuracy, as indicated by its mean square error (MSE).

4.2.1 Broad Area Ratio Estimator

The broad area ratio estimator (BARE) is one of the simplest and most straightforward forms of SAE. To derive this estimator, we use the direct estimate of the variable of interest for the broad area obtained from a survey and the small area population sourced from a population census or demographic estimate (ABS 2006).

Suppose we want to generate the total number of poor people in a municipality. The small area of interest is the municipality, and the available data at the provincial (broad area) level are direct estimates from surveys and population data for the small area. The number of poor people in the municipality can be calculated by applying the provincial poverty incidence to the municipality-level population. The BARE for the small area i^{th} is $\hat{Y}_i$:

$$\hat{Y}_i = \hat{\bar{Y}}_p \mathrm{N}_i \tag{4.3}$$

---

[9] MSE is an aggregate measure of precision and accuracy. It is expressed as the sum of the variance (as measure of precision) and square of bias (as measure of accuracy). Earlier, we noted that direct survey estimators are unbiased; hence, its MSE simply reduces to the variance of the estimator.

where $\hat{\bar{Y}}_p$ is the reliable direct estimator of the provincial area p and N_i is the total municipality-level population. From the survey sample, $\hat{\bar{Y}}_p$ can be calculated from $\dfrac{\hat{Y}_p}{\hat{N}_p}$, which is the proportion of the number of poor people in provincial area p to the total population in that province.

The major assumption is that the small areas share the same characteristics as the large area to generate unbiased estimates. In addition, producing reliable small area estimates requires calculation of the direct estimate for the large area from a survey with sufficiently large sample size. Together with direct estimators, BAREs can serve as references in confirming the results of small area estimates from more complicated methods.

Table 4.1 shows a simple example of how to calculate BARE estimates using a hypothetical survey and census data for Province X (i.e., the broad area). The poverty incidence in Province X is 46.27%, with a coefficient of variation of 9.8%. Additionally, Province X contains 23 small areas (municipalities) with sample sizes that are not large enough to generate reliable direct estimates.

Table 4.1: Population and Magnitude of Poor Population for Each Municipality in Province X

Municipality	Census Population	Poor Population (no.)
1	16,026	7,415
2	14,085	6,517
3	10,125	4,685
4	69,297	32,064
5	21,015	9,724
6	42,866	19,834
7	14,550	6,732
8	13,308	6,158
9	52,991	24,519
10	8,573	3,967
11	7,885	3,648
12	12,742	5,896
13	20,149	9,323
14	5,407	2,502
15	14,743	6,822
16	6,070	2,809
17	36,540	16,907
18	14,779	6,838
19	22,532	10,426
20	14,498	6,708
21	14,687	6,796
22	15,377	7,115
23	18,915	8,752

Source: Asian Development Bank estimates.

The data set for the estimation can be set up with the following command in R:

```
install.packages("dplyr", dependencies = TRUE)
library (readxl)
library(dplyr)
poverty_bare <-read_excel("poverty_bare.xlsx")
```

Given the data set, the BARE for municipal estimates in Province X can be obtained using the command

```
poverty_bare$povcount_mun <- poverty_bare$povrate_prov * poverty_bare$popn_mun
```

or

```
mutate (poverty_bare, povcount_mun = povrate_prov * popn_mun)
```

The BARE may also include additional auxiliary data (e.g., population counts by age and by sex) that correlate with the variable of interest and are available at the small area level. In the example given, the estimator may apply population by age and sex, and poverty rate to the municipality-level population classified by age and sex. The estimate for each small area population $\hat{Y}_i^u$ contained in each small area i is now a function of the direct estimator for category c in the large area p and counts of the population for each category. The superscipt u refers to the multivariate case having several subgroups of the population of interest. Thus,

$$\hat{Y}_i^u = \sum_c \frac{N_{ic}\hat{Y}_{pc}^u}{N_{pc}}, \tag{4.4}$$

where $\hat{Y}_{pc}^u$ is the direct estimate of poor population for Province p, N_{pc} is the total number of people in age-sex category c in Province p, and N_{ic} is the total number of people in age-sex category c in municipality level i.

4.2.2 (Synthetic) Calibration Methods

A simple model is used to synthetically produce small area statistics. Purcell and Kish (1979) described the *synthetic estimation* procedure as a technique that uses sample data to estimate, at some higher level of aggregation, the variable of interest for different subclasses of the population, then scales these estimates in proportion to the subclass of incidence within the small domains of interest. Because these estimates are not obtained directly from survey results, the estimates are referred to as synthetic estimates.

The procedure obtained unbiased estimates using survey results for a large area, and these unbiased estimates were used to derive estimates for subareas with the assumption that the small areas have the same characteristics as the large area. Hence, the method borrows information from similar small domains to increase the accuracy of the resulting estimates. The procedure also produces consistent estimates. The synthetic estimation procedure is generally simple and intuitive. It is easy to implement, because it applies to general sampling designs.

The structure of the data set for synthetic estimation can be visualized in a two-way table, where the rows represent the small areas indexed by *i* having values from 1 to *m* and the columns represent the subgroup levels, indexed by *g* having values from 1 to G (Table 4.2).

Table 4.2: Structure of Data Set for Synthetic Estimation

Small Area	Subgroup					
	1	2	...	*g*	...	G
1	Cell (1,1)	Cell (1,2)	...	Cell (1,*g*)	...	Cell (1,G)
2	Cell (2,1)	Cell (2,2)	...	Cell (2,*g*)	...	Cell (2,G)
:	:	:	:	:	:	:
i	Cell (*i*,1)	Cell (*i*,2)	...	Cell (*i*,*g*)	...	Cell (*i*,G)
:	:	:	:	:	:	:
m	Cell (*m*,1)	Cell (*m*,2)	...	Cell (*m*,*g*)	...	Cell (*m*,G)

An i,g^{th} cell represents a value at the gth level of the auxiliary variable in the ith small area. The value in each cell is said to be known and is usually denoted as X_{ig}. The variable of interest, usually denoted as Y is unknown and must be estimated for each small area. An estimate of Y for the ith small area is denoted by $\hat{Y}_i$. However, unbiased estimates for the variable of interest in the large area for subgroup g (denoted as $\hat{Y}_{.g}^D$) using survey results are assumed to be available for all subgroups. Using these available estimates, a

synthetic estimate of the variable of interest in the ith small area is computed as $\hat{Y}_i^S = \sum_{g=1}^{G} \frac{X_{ig}}{X_{.g}} \hat{Y}_{.g}^D$.

In some cases, an acceptable direct estimate (i.e., deemed precise) for the large area are also available for subpopulation groups (e.g., sex, age groups). A synthetic estimator (i.e., post-stratified estimator) can be constructed if population counts or auxiliary variable counts are available for subpopulation groups for specific small areas.

However, there is a potential bias associated with the synthetic estimator against the instability of a design-based or direct estimator. To correct for this bias, these two estimators are combined into one. The resulting estimator is the composite estimator, which strikes a balance between the bias of synthetic estimates and large variance of direct estimates. The direct estimate is deemed better when the sample size is large. Meanwhile, the synthetic estimate is better when the sample size is small or zero. Thus, the resulting composite estimator tends to have smaller bias and variance (Eurostat 2014).

The weighted average of the direct and synthetic estimator is one example of a composite estimator. It is expressed as

$$\hat{Y}_i^C = w_i \hat{Y}_{1i} + (1 - w_i)\hat{Y}_{2i}, \tag{4.5}$$

where $\hat{Y}_{1i}$ is a design-based or direct estimator, $\hat{Y}_{2i}$ is an indirect estimator, and w_i is a chosen weight with a value between 0 and 1. Usually, the design-unbiased or direct estimator $\hat{Y}_i$ is considered as $\hat{Y}_{1i}$, while the synthetic estimator $\hat{Y}_i^S$ is considered as $\hat{Y}_{2i}$. The assignment of weight depends on the sample size in the small area. Assign a bigger weight to the direct estimate if the sample size is large and assign bigger weight to the synthetic estimate if the sample size is small.

4.2.3 Survey Weight Reallocation Using Auxiliary Information from Statistical Neighbors

Let us suppose that we can identify statistical neighbors or a collection of small areas that are homogenous regarding our indicator of interest. Furthermore, let us also assume that we have a specific set of information that were collected via survey, but whose true values are also known from other data sources.

The principle behind survey weight reallocation is to artificially increase the sample size in a specific small area by including in the calculation information from sampled units from all statistical neighbors of the given small area. To do this, we reallocate the value of the survey weight originally attached to every sampled unit from the given small area to itself and to sampled units of its statistical neighbors (Figure 4.1).

Figure 4.1: Illustration of Weight Reallocation from Neighboring Subdomains

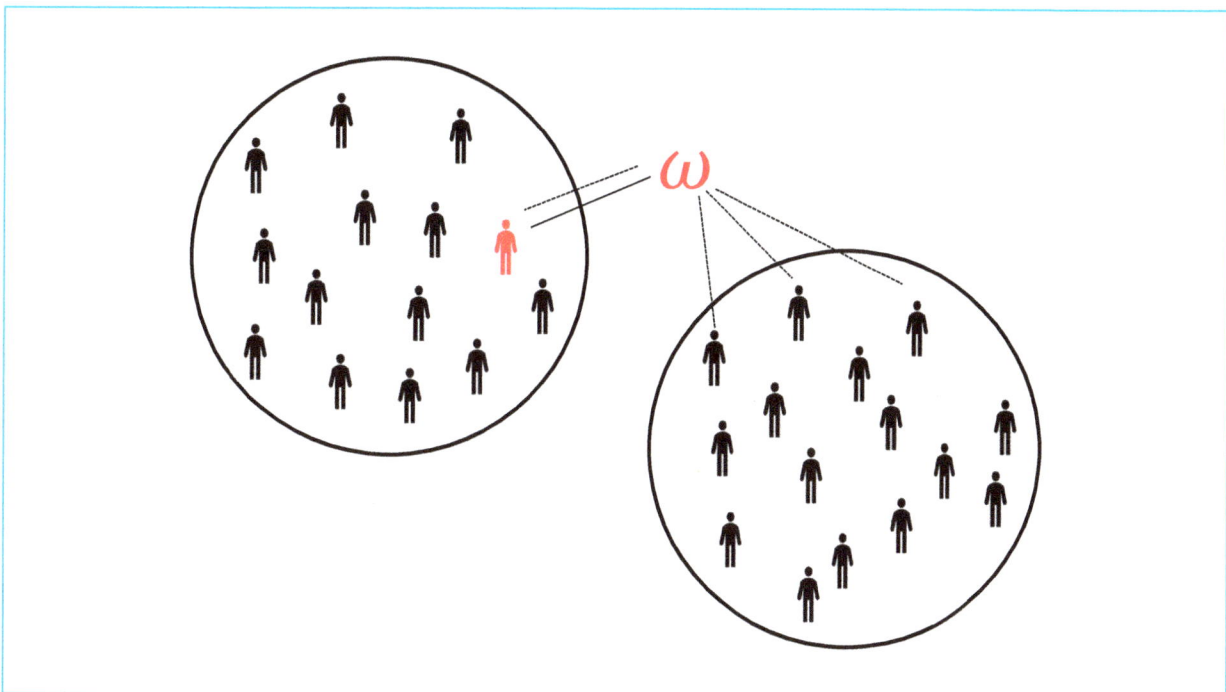

Source: Asian Development Bank.

There are several ways to reallocate survey weights. Schirm and Zaslavsky (1997) propose fitting a Poisson regression model using a two-step iterative procedure, which must satisfy two constraints:

$$\text{Constraint 1:} \quad \sum_d w_{id} = \omega_i \text{ for each i,}$$

$$\text{Constraint 2:} \quad \sum_d w_{id} x_{il} = X_{dl}$$

Survey weight reallocation implicitly changes the contribution of every sampled unit; however, the first constraint forces that its corresponding contribution to the overall estimate is fixed. The second constraint forces that all known totals are satisfied by weight-reallocated estimates. One can follow an iterative Newton-Raphson procedure in estimating the Poisson model parameters that will satisfy these constraints (Schirm and Zaslavsky 1997). Following Schirm and Zaslavsky's notations, and denoting with $\beta_{d(k)}$ and $\delta_{i(k)}$ the values of the reallocation model's unknown parameters, the iterative approach consists of the following steps:

At the kth iteration,

$$\text{Step 1: } \delta_{h(k)} = \ln\left(\frac{\omega_i}{\sum \exp(\beta_{d(k-1)} x_i)}\right)$$

$$\text{Step 2: } \beta_{d(k)} = \beta_{d(k-1)} + D_d^{-1} d_d \text{ for each } d,$$

where $D_d = \sum_i w_{id} x_i x_i'$ and $d_d = X_d - \sum_i w_{id} x_i$.

Note that the procedure assumes some initial values for $\beta_{d(0)}$ and $\delta_{i(0)}$.

The first step in the iterative procedure satisfies the constraint that the contribution of every sampled unit to the overall estimate for a particular characteristic of interest are the same, by substituting the expression for δ_{hk} in Step 1. Similarly, the second step is outlined to satisfy the second constraint that all known totals are met by the reallocated weighted estimates. As a general rule, we can stop the iterative procedure when the estimates converge (i.e., d_d) is sufficiently small.

A key advantage of this weight reallocation methodology over other SAE techniques is that it is not heavily dependent on which indicator needs estimation. Furthermore, aside from control totals, it is not necessary to compile data on covariates of the indicator of interest. However, a potential disadvantage of this weight reallocation strategy is the potential bias that it may induce, especially when the statistical neighbors are not homogeneous with respect to the indicator of interest.

In the two-step modeling process, two constraints must be satisfied:

- Reweighing must not change the total weight given to a sample unit across all subdomains. That is, at the domain level $\sum_s w_{hs} = w_h$ for each h, where w_h is the control weight (the original sample weight) of the sample unit.

- All control totals are satisfied for every subdomain. That is, $\sum_s w_{hs} x_{hi} = X_{si}$ for each s and i, where x_{hi} is the control total of the control variable in i in subdomain s.

The method is easy to implement, but computationally intense. It is said to be a little subjective in its choice of characteristics to be preserved in the process. The procedure is also subject to survey error and model error. It must satisfy the assumption that the neighboring subdomain from which the observed data are taken has the same level of outcome to the subdomain of interest (i.e., there is homogeneity of responses among the subdomains).

To implement survey weight reallocation using R software, we need to undertake some preliminary steps (e.g., installing packages and setting the working directory). For this example, we will import a Stata data set. Hence, we need to install the *readstata13* R package. We also need to install the *survey* package:

```
install.packages("readstata13", dependencies = TRUE)
install.packages("survey", dependencies = TRUE)
install.packages("openxlsx", dependencies = TRUE)
```

If these packages are already installed, we can use the following commands to make them active:

```
library(readstata13)
library(survey)
library(openxlsx)
```

Set the working directory and load the data set using the commands

```
setwd("working directory")
dataset <- read.dta13("data for weight reallocation.dta")
```

To generate variables needed for the Poisson model, sample commands include

```
import_iteration <- 20
prov_codes <- c(7, 36, 38, 66, 70)
factors <- c("famsize", "male", "educ1", "educ2", "educ3")
other_details <- c("regn", "prov", "stratum", "psu")
n <- length(factors)
m <- length(prov_codes)
obs <- nrow(dataset)
weight_hat_col <- c("weight_hat7", "weight_hat36", "weight_hat38", "weight_hat66", "weight_hat70")
```

The next step is to specify the survey design parameters:

```
svydataset <- svydesign(data = dataset,
            ids = ~1,
            strata = ~stratum,
            weights = ~weight,
            nest = TRUE)
```

To examine the control totals, use the following R commands:

```
controlprov_final <- matrix(ncol = n)
for (i in 1:m) {
  prov_subset <- subset(svydataset, prov == prov_codes[i])
  totals <- svytotal(~famsize + male + educ1 + educ2 + educ3, prov_subset)
  controlprov <- t(matrix(totals))
  controlprov_final <- rbind(controlprov_final, controlprov)
}
controlprov_final <- controlprov_final[2:(m + 1), ]
colnames(controlprov_final) <- factors
rownames(controlprov_final) <- prov_codes
```

Next, generate Poisson model in R:

```
beta_final <- matrix(ncol = n)
for (i in 1:m) {
  prov_subset <- subset(svydataset, prov == prov_codes[i])
  glm <- svyglm(formula = weight ~ famsize + male + educ1 + educ2 + educ3 - 1,
          family = quasipoisson(),
          design = prov_subset)
  print(summary(glm))
  beta <- t(matrix(glm$coefficients))
  beta_final <- rbind(beta_final, beta)
}
rm(beta, glm)
beta_final <- beta_final[2:(m + 1), ]
colnames(beta_final) <- factors
rownames(beta_final) <- prov_codes

iteration <- cbind(dataset[other_details], dataset[factors], original_weight = dataset$weight)

write.xlsx(x = iteration, file = "weight reallocation.xlsx", sheetName = "Iteration 0", row.names = FALSE)
```

The following commands show the iteration process needed to implement in R. For this case, we propose 20 iterations:

```
j <- 1
while (j <= 20) {
```

First, we generate a matrix for each observation, containing all control variables.

```
X <- as.matrix(dataset[factors])
```

Next, we generate matrices containing the product of the coefficients and control variables for each observation to represent the exponent in the formula in Step 1.

```
Xprov <- X %*% t(beta_final)
Y <- rowSums(Xprov)
```

We then calculate delta_h.

```
deltah <- log(dataset$weight / rowSums(exp(Xprov)))
```

We also calculate the reallocated weights, using the Step 1 formula.

```
weight_hat <- exp(Xprov + deltah)
colnames(weight_hat) <- weight_hat_col
```

Next, we compute D_prov and the second term of d_prov for observation 1, from the Step 2 formula. We also calculate D_prov and the second term of d_prov from observation 2 up to last observation, from the Step 2 formula.

```
Wprov <- weight_hat
Dprov <- matrix(0, nrow = n, ncol = n)
dprov_temp <- matrix(0, ncol = n)
matlist_prov <- list(Dprov)
matlistprov_temp <- list(dprov_temp)
for (i in 2:m) {
  matlist_prov[[i]] <- Dprov
  matlistprov_temp[[i]] <- dprov_temp
}
for (i in 1:obs) {
  for (k in 1:m) {
    dummy_1 <- Wprov[i, k] * X[i, ] %*% t(X[i, ])
    matlist_prov[[k]] <- matlist_prov[[k]] + dummy_1
    dummy_2 <- Wprov[i, k] * X[i, ]
    matlistprov_temp[[k]] <- matlistprov_temp[[k]] + dummy_2
  }
}
for (k in 1:m) {
  dprov_temp <- rbind(dprov_temp, matlistprov_temp[[k]])
}
dprov_temp <- dprov_temp[2:(m + 1), ]
colnames(dprov_temp) <- factors
```

We compute d_prov from the Step 2 formula.

```
ddprov <- controlprov_final - dprov_temp
```

We calculate the formula for beta in the Step 2 formula.

```
for (k in 1:m) {
   beta_final[k, ] <- beta_final[k, ] + solve(matlist_prov[[k]]) %*% ddprov[k, ]
 }

Yprov <-  X %*% t(beta_final)
```

Next, we recalculate the reallocated weights using the Step 1 formula, with coefficients derived from the Step 2 formula for beta.

```
weight_hat <- exp(Yprov + deltah)
colnames(weight_hat) <- weight_hat_col

if (j <= import_iteration) {
 iteration <- cbind(dataset[other_details],
          dataset[factors],
          original_weight = dataset$weight,
          weight_hat)
 iteration$constraint2_weightcheck <- iteration$original_weight - (iteration$weight_hat7 + iteration$weight_hat36 +
                          iteration$weight_hat38 + iteration$weight_hat66 +
                          iteration$weight_hat70)
 iteration$control_famsize_orig <- iteration$famsize * iteration$original_weight
 iteration$control_male_orig <- iteration$male * iteration$original_weight
 iteration$control_educ1_orig <- iteration$educ1 * iteration$original_weight
 iteration$control_educ2_orig <- iteration$educ2 * iteration$original_weight
 iteration$control_educ3_orig <- iteration$educ3 * iteration$original_weight

 constraint1_orig <- iteration %>%
  group_by(prov) %>%
  summarise(famsize_total_orig = sum(control_famsize_orig),
      male_total_orig = sum(control_male_orig),
      educ1_total_orig = sum(control_educ1_orig),
      educ2_total_orig = sum(control_educ2_orig),
      educ3_total_orig = sum(control_educ3_orig))

 constraint1_rwght <- data.frame()
 for (i in 1:m) {
  control_rwght <- data.frame(iteration$famsize * iteration[10 + i],
            iteration$male * iteration[10 + i],
            iteration$educ1 * iteration[10 + i],
            iteration$educ2 * iteration[10 + i],
            iteration$educ3 * iteration[10 + i])
  colnames(control_rwght) <- paste0("control_", factors, "_rwght_", prov_codes[i])
  constraint1_rwght <- rbind(constraint1_rwght, colSums(control_rwght))
  iteration <- cbind(iteration, control_rwght)
  i <- i + 1
 }
 colnames(constraint1_rwght) <- paste0(factors, "_total_rwght")
 constraint1_rwght <- cbind(prov = constraint1_orig$prov, constraint1_rwght)

 constraint1_controlcheck <- constraint1_orig[-1] - constraint1_rwght[-1]
 colnames(constraint1_controlcheck) <- paste0(factors, "_totals_check")
 constraint1_controlcheck <- cbind(prov = constraint1_orig$prov, constraint1_controlcheck)

wb <- loadWorkbook(file = "weight reallocation.xlsx")
 addWorksheet(wb, paste("Iteration", j))
 writeData(wb, sheet = paste("Iteration", j), iteration, rowNames = FALSE)

 writeData(wb, sheet = paste("Iteration", j), "Original Control Totals", rowNames = FALSE,
     startCol = length(iteration) + 2, startRow = 2)
 writeData(wb, sheet = paste("Iteration", j), constraint1_orig, rowNames = FALSE,
     startCol = length(iteration) + 2, startRow = 3)

 writeData(wb, sheet = paste("Iteration", j), "Reweighted Control Totals", rowNames = FALSE,
     startCol = length(iteration) + 2, startRow = nrow(constraint1_orig) + 5)
 writeData(wb, sheet = paste("Iteration", j), constraint1_rwght, rowNames = FALSE,
     startCol = length(iteration) + 2, startRow = nrow(constraint1_orig) + 6)

 writeData(wb, sheet = paste("Iteration", j), "Control Totals Difference", rowNames = FALSE,
     startCol = length(iteration) + 2, startRow = nrow(constraint1_orig) + nrow(constraint1_rwght) + 8)
 writeData(wb, sheet = paste("Iteration", j), constraint1_controlcheck, rowNames = FALSE,
     startCol = length(iteration) + 2, startRow = nrow(constraint1_orig) + nrow(constraint1_rwght) + 9)
 saveWorkbook(wb, "weight reallocation.xlsx", overwrite = TRUE)
}

j <- j + 1
}
```

The next step is to re-specify survey design parameters:

```
svydataset <- svydesign(data = dataset,
            ids = ~1,
            strata = ~stratum,
            weights = ~weight,
            nest = TRUE)
controlprov_final <- matrix(ncol = n)
for (i in 1:m) {
  prov_subset <- subset(svydataset, prov == prov_codes[i])
  totals <- svytotal(~famsize + male + educ1 + educ2 + educ3, prov_subset)
  controlprov <- t(matrix(totals))
  controlprov_final <- rbind(controlprov_final, controlprov)
}
controlprov_final <- controlprov_final[2:(m + 1), ]}
```

We also need to specify the reweighted survey design parameters using the following R commands:

```
dummy_2 <- weight_hat
colnames(dummy_2) <- weight_hat_col
dataset <- cbind(dataset, dummy_2)
rwghtdctlprov_final <- matrix(ncol = n)

for (i in 1:m) {
  svydataset <- svydesign(data = dataset,
              ids = ~1,
              strata = ~stratum,
              weights = ~dataset[, 739 + i],
              nest = TRUE)
  prov_subset <- subset(svydataset, prov == prov_codes[i])
  totals <- svytotal(~famsize + male + educ1 + educ2 + educ3, prov_subset)
  rwghtdctlprov <- t(matrix(totals))
  rwghtdctlprov_final <- rbind(rwghtdctlprov_final, rwghtdctlprov)
}
rwghtdctlprov_final <- rwghtdctlprov_final[2:(m + 1), ]
```

Compare control totals based on original survey weights and weights after reallocation using the following commands:

```
for (i in 1:m) {
  print(controlprov_final[, i])
  print(rwghtdctlprov_final[, i])
}
```

Finally, we must check that for each observation, the original weight is equal to the total reallocated weights. The minimum and maximum values should be close to zero.

```
wgtdiff <- dataset$weight - rowSums(weight_hat)
summary(wgtdiff)}
```

4.3 Small Area Estimation Using Regression-Based Models

In this section, we discuss the model-based approaches of estimating small area statistics using data from different sources like nationwide surveys, census, administrative records, and even data sets that are classified as Big Data. Such approaches, which generally use regression-based models, include regression-synthetic, empirical best linear unbiased prediction (EBLUP), empirical Bayes, and the hierarchical Bayes techniques. Another popular model-based approach, is the estimation method of Elbers, Lanjouw, and Lanjouw (2003).[10]

Model-based approach methodology includes an error structure component that allows measurement of local variation among small areas. Models can generate efficient estimates, and sample data can validate the models. This indirect method has gained popularity because it can handle complex cases such as cross-sectional and time-series data. Unlike synthetic and composite estimators, the estimates obtained in this method include specific measures of variability.

The models used in this method can be either linear or nonlinear. The more common and easily used is the general linear model. The linear model has two components: one is derived from the survey data, and the other from the modeling process. Specifically, the first component has an error term (e) that results from the sampling process involved in data collection, while the second component has an error term (u) that accounts for the modeling process. Thus, a general linear mixed model has the following form:

$$\hat{Y}_i^D = \mathbf{x_i^T}\boldsymbol{\beta} + u_i + e_i, \qquad (4.7)$$

where $\hat{Y}_i^D$ is a direct estimate for the ith small area; $\mathbf{x_i^T}$ is the transpose vector of the observed values at the ith small area of the predictors identified in the model, and $\boldsymbol{\beta}$ is the p-vector of regression parameters. As identified previously, the model has two independent errors: (i) the sampling error e_i, which is assumed to be independent across the small areas i and has a mean zero and common variance, $\sigma_{e_i}^2$, and (ii) the model error u_i independent of the sampling error e_i which is also assumed to be independent across the small areas i and has a mean zero and common variance, σ_u^2.

This indirect method, which uses the model-based approach, follows the modeling process to find the "best" predicting model for generating the estimates. The "best" predicting model must satisfy the assumptions of the model being fitted to generate valid estimates. Likewise, the model must also possess the "good" properties of a statistical model (e.g., model adequacy and significant regression coefficients). In relation to the estimates obtained using the predicting model, estimates must possess "good" statistical properties such as accuracy, precision, and reliability.

---

[10] ELL is a World Bank poverty mapping methodology, which is a popular SAE application in more than 70 countries. Other than poverty and inequality maps, the ELL technique is also used in generating health and nutrition maps in developing countries (Van Der Weide 2017).

4.3.1   Regression-Synthetic Estimation

Regression-synthetic estimation is a regression-based estimation technique, which uses a linear model applicable for a quantitative dependent variable and a weighted least squares estimator of $\boldsymbol{\beta}$, the vector of regression coefficients. We estimate local area parameters using a multiple linear regression, assuming that the variable of interest is linearly dependent with the auxiliary variables, and applying independent variables obtained from either censuses or administrative records.

An area-level regression-synthetic estimator, which is defined at the small area-level and relates the direct estimates and the area-level auxiliary information, is based on the model

$$\mathbf{Y} = \boldsymbol{X}^T\boldsymbol{\beta} + \boldsymbol{u} + \boldsymbol{e}, \tag{4.8}$$

where $\mathbf{Y}$ is an m x 1 vector of the parameter of interest (e.g., total, mean, or proportion);

$\quad \boldsymbol{X}^T$ is an m x p matrix of area-level auxiliary variables;
$\quad \boldsymbol{\beta}$ is a p x 1 vector of regression parameters;
$\quad \boldsymbol{u}$ is an m x 1 vector of area-level residual term; and
$\quad \boldsymbol{e}$ is an m x 1 vector of pooled within-area residual term.

We assume that $\boldsymbol{u} + \boldsymbol{e}$ is independently and identically distributed with mean 0 and variance $\boldsymbol{\sigma_u^2} + \boldsymbol{\sigma_e^2}$ (i.e. $\boldsymbol{u} + \boldsymbol{e} \sim (\boldsymbol{0}, \boldsymbol{\sigma_u^2} + \boldsymbol{\sigma_e^2})$) and obtain a regression-synthetic estimator when auxiliary variables (also known as covariates) with total or mean values are available only for the target small areas.

We express the regression-synthetic estimator based on the area-level model as

$$\widehat{Y}_i = \boldsymbol{X}_i^T\widetilde{\boldsymbol{\beta}} \tag{4.9}$$

where $\widehat{\mathbf{Y}}_i$ is the predicted or estimated parameter of interest for area/domain i,

$\quad \boldsymbol{X}^T$ is a 1 x p vector of auxiliary information about the area/domain i, and

$\quad \widetilde{\boldsymbol{\beta}}$ is a p x 1 vector of the weighted least squares estimator of the regression parameters $\boldsymbol{\beta}$.

Thus, we can derive the regression-synthetic estimator by fitting a regression model to the available data in the small areas and using the model to determine with the predicted values, which serve as the regression-synthetic estimates. In other words, the predicted values $\widehat{Y}_i$, obtained from $\boldsymbol{x}_i^T\widetilde{\boldsymbol{\beta}}$, are the regression-synthetic estimates of $\boldsymbol{Y}_i$. Meanwhile, $\widetilde{\boldsymbol{\beta}}$ is the weighted least squares estimator of $\boldsymbol{\beta}$ and can be expressed as

$$\widetilde{\boldsymbol{\beta}} = \left(\sum \frac{X_iX_i^T}{\widehat{\sigma_u^2}+\widehat{\sigma_e^2}}\right)^{-1}\left(\sum \frac{X_i\widehat{Y}_i}{\widehat{\sigma_u^2}+\widehat{\sigma_e^2}}\right), \tag{4.10}$$

where $\widehat{\sigma_u^2}$ and $\widehat{\sigma_e^2}$ are the estimates of the variances of the model and sampling errors, respectively. A simple method of moment estimator $\widehat{\sigma_u^2}$,proposed by Prassad and Rao (1990), is expressed as $\widehat{\sigma_u^2} = \max(\widehat{\sigma_u^2}, 0)$, where

$$\hat{\sigma}_u^2 = \frac{1}{m-p}\left[\sum\left(\hat{Y}_i - \boldsymbol{X}_i^T\widetilde{\boldsymbol{\beta}}\right)^2 - \sum \hat{\sigma}_{e_i}^2\left(1-h_{ii}\right)\right], \tag{4.11}$$

where $h_{ii} = X_i^T \left(\sum X_i X_i^T \right)^{-1} X_i$; m is the number of small areas; and p is the number of predictors.

Performance of the regression-synthetic estimator depends on the relationship between the area-level parameter of interest and the vector of auxiliary variable. The success of using this estimation technique for small areas mostly relies on getting good predictors resulting to smaller model variance. Hence, it is important to conduct an assessment and validation of the model and test whether the assumptions required for regression analysis and the adequacy of the model are satisfied. In identifying the auxiliary variables to include in the model as predictors, we can conduct correlation analysis and assess their statistical and practical significance. To find the best regression model, we may consider model selection procedures such as stepwise regression.

A model is deemed "best" if it satisfies the following criteria:

- the model has the most parsimonious set of predictors and the optimum predictive power;
- assumptions regarding normality of errors, independence of errors, homoscedasticity of error terms, and 0 mean error are satisfied; and
- there is a consistent relationship between the predictors and the dependent variable based on earlier studies.

Selecting the set of covariates that best explain the between-area variation of the variable of interest can result in smaller mean squared error. Thus, we need to assess the regression-synthetic estimates through the mean square of the predicted values. This is based on the value of the mean square error (*mse*) of the predicted model and is computed as

$$mse\left(\hat{Y_i}\right) = mse\left(X_i^T \left(X_i^T X_i\right)^{-1} X_i\right),$$
(4.12)

while the coefficient of variation of the estimate is computed as

$$cv\left(\hat{Y_i}\right) = \frac{\sqrt{mse(\hat{Y_i})}}{\hat{Y_i}} \times 100\%.$$
(4.13)

Moreover, we can construct a 95% confidence interval (C.I.) using the equation

$$C.I. = \hat{Y_i} \pm 1.96 \sqrt{mse\left(\hat{Y_i}\right)}.$$
(4.14)

For illustration, consider generating regression-synthetic estimates of relative poverty at the provincial level, which is the proportion of households with income below 50% of the national median income. We obtain the direct estimates of the proportion of Filipino households with income below 50% of the national median income and their corresponding measure of precision.

We use data sets from the income and expenditure survey and the census of population and housing. The income and expenditure survey is a nationwide survey of households, which is the main source of household income and expenditures data that include, among others, sources of cash and in-kind income and the levels of consumption by item of expenditure. On the other hand, the census, which is a complete enumeration of households in the country, collects information on the characteristics of the population and their housing units. The provincial-level variables in the census data set serve as auxiliary information for model building.

We generate direct estimates of the proportion of households with income below 50% of median income and obtain their corresponding measures of precision using the survey data set. Note that in direct estimation, we use the weights of the sampling design employed in the survey. Let the subscript i denote the ith province and the subscript j denote the jth household. A direct estimator of the proportion (expressed in percentage) for the ith province is given by

$$\hat{P}_i^D = \frac{\sum_h \sum_a \sum_j w_{haj} y_{i-haj}}{\sum_h \sum_a \sum_j w_{haj} x_{i-haj}} \times 100\% = \frac{\hat{Y}_i}{\hat{X}_i} \times 100\%, \qquad (4.15)$$

where y_{i-haj} is equal to 1 if the jth household in the ath primary sampling unit (PSU) in the hth stratum of the ith province has per capita income below 50% of the national median income and to 0 otherwise;

w_{haj} is the final weight associated for the jth household in the ath PSU in the hth stratum of the ith province. It represents the number of households in the population represented by the jth household;

x_{i-haj} is equal to 1 if the jth household in the ath PSU in the hth stratum of the ith province belongs to the ith province and to 0 otherwise;

$\hat{Y}_i$ is the direct estimator of the total number of households in the ith province with per capita income below 50% of the national income; and

$\hat{X}_i$ is the direct estimator of the total number of households in the ith province.

The direct estimator is a ratio estimator and usually biased. Hence, it is appropriate to compute a measure of precision and accuracy (e.g., mean square of error). Cochran (1977) explained the overall measure of accuracy and precision as

$$\widehat{mse}(\hat{P}_i^D) = (\hat{P}_i^D)^2 \left[\frac{\hat{V}(\hat{Y}_i)}{(\hat{Y}_i)^2} + \frac{\hat{V}(\hat{X}_i)}{(\hat{X}_i)^2} - \frac{2\widehat{COV}(\hat{Y}_i, \hat{X}_i)}{(\hat{Y}_i \hat{X}_i)} \right]$$

where $\hat{V}(\hat{Y}_i) = \sum_{h \in i} \frac{1}{a_h(a_h-1)} \sum_a \left(y_{i-ha} - \frac{\hat{Y}_{i-h}}{a_h} \right); \hat{V}(\hat{X}_i) = \sum_{h \in i} \frac{1}{a_h(a_h-1)} \sum_a \left(x_{i-ha} - \frac{\hat{X}_{i-h}}{a_h} \right)$

and $\widehat{COV}(\hat{Y}_{i_i}, \hat{X}_{i_i}) = \sum_{h \in i} \frac{1}{a_h(a_h-1)} \sum_a \left(y_{i-ha} - \frac{\hat{Y}_{i-h}}{a_h} \right) \left(x_{i-ha} - \frac{\hat{X}_{i-h}}{a_h} \right),$

while a measure of reliability of the direct estimates is given by

$$cv(\hat{P}_i^D) = \frac{\sqrt{mse(\hat{P}_i^D)}}{\hat{P}_i^D} \times 100\%. \qquad (4.16)$$

To do the regression-synthetic estimation using R software, we need to undertake some preliminary steps, like setting a working directory and installing some R packages that were not installed previously.

Otherwise, we just activate the packages before the estimation begins. The working directory, which contains all files needed in the estimation, can be set using the command

```
setwd("working directory")
```

If it is necessary to install the needed packages, use the command "*install.*" The required R packages are **MASS, readxl, leaps, lmtest, car, dplyr,** and **writexl**. See Appendix 1 for descriptions of these packages.

```
install.packages(c("MASS","readxl","leaps","lmtest",
"car","dplyr","writexl","dplyr"), dependencies = TRUE)
```

If these packages are already installed, we can use the following commands:

```
library(MASS)
library(readxl)
library(leaps)
library(lmtest)
library(car)
library(writexl)
library(dplyr)
```

Step 1: Follow the modeling steps (Appendix 3) to identify the dependent variable and possible predictors (i.e., independent variables). In the regression-synthetic model, the direct estimate of the provincial proportion of households with income below 50% of the national median income is the dependent variable. On the other hand, the predictors refer to characteristics of the provinces identified in the census data set. Some examples of predicting variables include the provincial proportion of households residing in housing units with roofs made of strong materials, the provincial proportion of female-headed households, and the provincial proportion of household heads who are at least high school graduates, to name a few, together with other similarly defined variables.

Step 2: Specify the functional form. The linear regression model needs to be fitted with the direct estimates as the dependent variable.

$$\hat{P}_i^D = \beta_0 + \beta_1 X_{i1} + ... + \beta_p X_{ip} + u_i + e_i, \qquad i = 1,2,..., m .\qquad (4.17)$$

Step 3: Organize the data set. For this illustration, we use the data set (filename: **hiescph.xlsx**) from the working directory:

```
rel_poverty<-read_excel("hiescph.xlsx")
```

The data set **hiescph.xlsx** (Appendix 2) contains the provincial direct estimates of the proportion of households with income below 50% of the national median income as well as the auxiliary variables obtained from the census. We can view the data set in R using the command

```
view(rel_poverty)
```

Step 4: Identify the appropriate modeling estimation procedure. Since the model to be fitted is linear, the least squares estimation procedure is appropriate. Using least squares estimation, the "best" model can be identified as stated in Step 5.

Step 5: Use stepwise regression to identify the "best" model with the following command:

```
rel_povertyv2<-rel_poverty[-c(1:12,14:17)]
null<-lm(direct_female~1, data=rel_povertyv2)
full<-lm(direct_female~., data=rel_povertyv2)
best<-step(null, scope = list(upper=full),data=rel_povertyv2, direction="both")
summary(best)
```

Note that the "best" model generated by the software may not always be considered as the final model for the estimation.

Step 6: Perform residual analysis twice in regression-synthetic estimation when (i) implementing an ordinary least squares (OLS) estimation, and (ii) using weighted least squares estimation. In ordinary least squares estimation, there is a possibility that some assumptions are not satisfied, but the weighted least squares method can result in residuals satisfying the assumptions.

Using the identified predictors in the "best" model (Step 5), we fit an OLS model using predictors with direct estimates as the dependent variable. If the "best" model's predictors are (i) the proportion of persons with at least high school education in the province (all_atleasthh) and (ii) the proportion of housing units with walls made of strong materials in the province (wall_strong_oldp), we then implement OLS through the commands

```
model.1 <- lm(direct_female ~ all_atleasthh + wall_strong_oldp, data = rel_povertyv2)
summary(model.1)
```

After fitting the OLS model, we can perform residual analysis to check for satisfaction of the underlying assumptions of the linear model (Appendix 3, Section 3).

Using the following commands, respectively, we also conduct a Durbin-Watson test for testing independence of errors, a Breusch-Pagan test for assessing homogeneity of variance, and a Wilk-Shapiro test for determining whether the residuals follow the normal distribution:

```
durbinWatsonTest(model.1)
```

```
ncvTest(model.1)
```

```
res1<-residuals(model.1)
shapiro.test(res1)
```

On the other hand, we use the variance inflation factor (VIF) to check for the presence of multicollinearity, using the command

```
vif(model.1)
```

Note which assumptions are satisfied and which are not. Next, fit the model using weighted least squares (WLS) on the same set of predictors and dependent variable, which we can do using the following command:

```
wts <- 1/fitted(lm(abs(residuals(model.1)) ~ all_atleasthh + wall_strong_oldp, data = rel_povertyv2))^2
model.2 <- lm(direct_female ~ all_atleasthh + wall_strong_oldp, data = rel_povertyv2, weights=wts)
summary(model.2)
```

We then implement residual analysis to check on the assumptions of the model, using the commands identified earlier. But this time, the assumptions of the model must all be satisfied. Otherwise, remedial measures are done to obtain a predicting model that will fully satisfy the assumptions.

Step 7: From the "best" fitted model obtained in Step 6, generate the predicted proportions and the corresponding standard errors and merge it to the original data set using the following commands:

```
syn_reg_est <- predict(model.2, rel_povertyv2, se.fit=TRUE)
syn_reg_data <- cbind(rel_poverty, syn_reg_est)
```

Step 8: Generate the estimates' corresponding coefficient of variation and confidence intervals using following commands to assess the statistical properties of the estimates:

```
cv_reg_est <- (syn_reg_data$se.fit/ syn_reg_data$fit) * 100
ll_reg_est <- syn_reg_data$fit - (1.96* syn_reg_data$se.fit)
ul_reg_est <- syn_reg_data$fit + (1.96* syn_reg_data$se.fit)
```

To present the results in a spreadsheet format, we can export them to Excel using the following commands:

```
syn_reg_finaldata <- cbind(syn_reg_data, cv_reg_est, ll_reg_est, ul_reg_est)
rename(syn_reg_finaldata, regsynth=fit, se_regsynth=se.fit)
View(syn_reg_finaldata)
write_xlsx(syn_reg_finaldata, "syn_reg_finaldata.xlsx")
```

Regression-synthetic estimates are available in the Excel file **syn_reg_finaldata.xlsx** with variable name **regsynth**. Moreover, the variable names for the estimates' standard error, the coefficient of variation, and the lower limit and upper limits are **se_regsynth**, **cv_reg_est**, **ll_reg_est**, and **ul_reg_est**, respectively. See Appendix 2 for a description of this data set.

4.3.2 Empirical Best Linear Unbiased Prediction Estimation

In regression-synthetic estimation, we implement the first half of empirical best linear unbiased prediction (EBLUP) estimation because the estimator in EBLUP is a composite estimator. As described earlier, a composite estimator is a weighted combination of two estimators: the direct or design-based estimator and the synthetic estimator (see Chapter IV, Section 4.2.2). In this case, the EBLUP estimator is a weighted combination of design-based estimator and regression-synthetic estimator.

Rao (2003) defined the EBLUP estimator as a weighted combination of two estimators, which is written as:

$$\hat{Y}_i^{EBLUP} = \gamma_i \hat{Y}_i^D + (1 - \gamma_i) \boldsymbol{X}_i^T \tilde{\boldsymbol{\beta}}, \tag{4.18}$$

where $\hat{Y}_i^D$ is the design-based or direct estimator, $\boldsymbol{X}_i^T \tilde{\boldsymbol{\beta}}$ is the regression-synthetic estimator, and $\gamma_i = \dfrac{\hat{\sigma}_u^2}{\hat{\sigma}_u^2 + \hat{\sigma}_{e_i}^2}$ is the shrinkage factor, or the weight of the direct estimator. The shrinkage factor can be computed as the ratio of $\hat{\sigma}_u^2$ to the total variance, $\hat{\sigma}_u^2 + \hat{\sigma}_{e_i}^2$, i.e., $\gamma_i = \dfrac{\hat{\sigma}_u^2}{\hat{\sigma}_u^2 + \hat{\sigma}_{e_i}^2}$. Weight γ_i is a value ranging from 0 to 1, which can also be defined so that if the variance $\hat{\sigma}_{e_i}^2$ is small, more weight is given to the direct estimate than the regression-synthetic. However, when the direct estimate is not reliable, more weight is given to the regression-synthetic estimator. Note that γ_i is chosen to minimize the mean square error of $\hat{Y}_i^{EBLUP}$. Moreover, $\hat{Y}_i^{EBLUP}$ is the regression-synthetic estimate for small areas without sampled units because it is impossible to derive direct estimates with no observations for given small areas.

Prasad and Rao (1990) approximated the unbiased estimator of the mean square error of the EBLUP estimator $\hat{Y}_i^{EBLUP}$. This is given as

$$mse\left(\hat{Y}_i^{EBLUP}\right) = \gamma_i \hat{\sigma}_{e_i}^2 + (1 - \gamma_i)^2 \boldsymbol{X}_i^T \left[\sum \frac{\boldsymbol{X}_i \boldsymbol{X}_i^T}{\hat{\sigma}_u^2 + \hat{\sigma}_{e_i}^2}\right]^{-1} \boldsymbol{X}_i + \frac{\hat{\sigma}_{e_i}^2}{\left(\hat{\sigma}_u^2 + \hat{\sigma}_{e_i}^2\right)^3} 4m^{-2} \sum \left(\hat{\sigma}_u^2 + \hat{\sigma}_{e_i}^2\right)^2. \tag{4.19}$$

The measure of reliability of estimates can be computed using the formula

$$cv\left(\hat{Y}_i^{EBLUP}\right) = \frac{\sqrt{mse\left(\hat{Y}_i^{EBLUP}\right)}}{\hat{Y}_i^{EBLUP}} \times 100\%. \tag{4.20}$$

Likewise, a 95% confidence interval (C.I.) can be constructed using the equation

$$C.I. = \hat{Y}_i^{EBLUP} \mp 1.96 \sqrt{mse\left(\hat{Y}_i^{EBLUP}\right)}. \tag{4.21}$$

An R sae-package developed by Molina and Marhuenda (2015) can be used to do the EBLUP estimation. It can be installed as one of the R packages needed for the estimation. Similar to the preliminary steps in regression-synthetic estimation, the working directory must be set and certain R packages must be installed. The packages for EBLUP estimation include **sae**, **readxl**, and **writexl**. See Appendix 1 for the descriptions of these packages.

```
install.packages(c("sae","readxl","writexl"), dependencies = TRUE)

library(sae)
library(readxl)
library(writexl)
```

The results of the regression-synthetic estimation will be used as inputs in EBLUP estimation. Thus, the data set for the estimation can be set up with the following command:

```
data_eblup <-read_excel("syn_reg_finaldata.xlsx")
```

The data set **syn_reg_finaldata.xlsx** contains the provincial direct estimates of the proportion of households with income below 50% of the national median income as well as the auxiliary variables from the census. See Appendix 2 for a description of this data set. We can view the data set in R using the following command:

```
View(data_eblup)
```

The next step is to generate EBLUP estimates of the proportion of households with income below 50% of the national median income, together with MSE estimates obtained from regression-synthetic estimation using the Fay and Herriot (FH) area level model.[11] Using functions eblupFH() and mseFH() in the **sae** R package, calculate small area estimates and corresponding analytical MSE estimates under the FH model, respectively (Molina and Marhuenda 2015).

Given the data set, EBLUP estimates can be obtained using the command

```
attach(data_eblup)
data_eblup2<-data_eblup[-c(9,84),]
attach(data_eblup2)
eblup_est <- eblupFH(direct_female ~ all_atleasthh + wall_strong_oldp,
se_direct^2, method = "REML", MAXITER = 100, PRECISION = 0.0001)
```

On the other hand, the calculated MSEs of the EBLUP estimates can be obtained using the command

```
mse_eblup_est <- mseFH(direct ~ all_atleasthh + wall_strong_oldp,
se_direct^2, method = "REML", MAXITER = 100, PRECISION = 0.0001)
```

To generate the estimates' corresponding coefficient of variation and confidence intervals, use the following commands:

---

[11] Fay and Herriot introduced this kind of model in 1979. These models are essential if unit (element) level data are not available.

```
eblup_data <- eblup_est$eblup
se_eblup_est <- sqrt(mse_eblup_est$mse)
cv_eblup <- 100* sqrt(mse_eblup_est$mse)/ mse_eblup_est$est$eblup
ll_eblup_est <- mse_eblup_est$est$eblup - (1.96* sqrt(mse_eblup_est$mse))
ul_eblup_est <- mse_eblup_est$est$eblup + (1.96* sqrt(mse_eblup_est$mse))
```

The results of the EBLUP estimation can be exported to an Excel using the following command:

```
eblup_finaldata <- cbind(data_eblup2, se_eblup_est, cv_eblup, ll_eblup_est, ul_eblup_est)
View(eblup_finaldata)
write_xlsx(eblup_finaldata, "eblup_finaldata.xlsx")
```

The EBLUP estimates are available in the Excel file **eblup_finaldata.xlsx** with variable name **eblup_data**. The description of this data set is provided in Appendix 2. Moreover, the variable names for the estimates' standard error, coefficient of variation, and lower limit and upper limits are **se_eblup_est, cv_eblup, ll_eblup_est**, and **ul_eblup_est**, respectively.

4.3.3   Poisson Regression Estimation

In a classical regression framework, we are interested in modeling a continuous response variable as a function of one or more predictor variables. However, the response of interest in many estimation problems is not continuous, but discrete in nature (i.e., the response variable takes only nonnegative integer values or counts). A natural stochastic model for such cases is the Poisson regression model. This model assumes that the response variable Y, which refers to the number of occurrences of the event of interest, has a Poisson distribution with probability mass function:

$$P(Y = y) = \frac{e^{-\lambda}\lambda^y}{y!}, \qquad y = 0, 1, 2, \dots, \qquad (4.22)$$

where λ is the intensity or rate parameter.

A Poisson model is analogous to an ordinary linear regression, but models the natural log of the response variable as a linear function of the predictors rather than modeling Y as a linear function of the predictors. Hence, when using Poisson regression model in small area estimation, the log of the expected counts of the variable of interest in the ith small area unit, $\hat{Y}_i^P$ is expressed as a linear function of a set of predictors (X) and is given by the log linear model

$$\log\left(\hat{Y}_i^P\right) = X_i^T \hat{\beta} + \mu_i, \qquad i = 1,2,\dots m, \qquad (4.23)$$

where X_i^T is a $1 \times p$ vector of auxiliary count data about the ith small area unit;

$\hat{\beta}$ is the Poisson regression estimator of a $p \times 1$ vector of regression parameters, denoted by β; and

μ_i is a vector of independent random errors which are distributed with mean zero and variance-covariance matrix expressed as $\sigma^2 I$.

Equivalently, this loglinear model can also be expressed as $\hat{Y}_i^P = e^{X_i^T \hat{\beta} + \mu_i}$.

Note that one of the most important assumptions of the Poisson regression model is the equality between its mean and variance. If this assumption is violated, the data may not fit the model and the obtained standard errors may be consistent. However, in real-life data the variance of count variables is often greater than the mean, hence violating the assumption. Thus, Cameron and Trivedi (2009) suggested obtaining robust standard errors for the parameter estimation to regulate any violation of the said assumption.

As is the case for all modeling procedures, the appropriateness of the fitted regression model must be examined before it is used for prediction (i.e., a measure of the overall fit of the model must be computed by comparing either (i) the actual values with the model-predicted values or (ii) a model to other models). A commonly used measure is the deviance statistic (D), which can be computed as

$$D = 2\sum_{i=1}^{m}\left[y_i \log\left(\frac{y_i}{\exp\{X_i^T \hat{\beta}\}}\right) - \left(y_i - \exp\{X_i^T \hat{\beta}\}\right)\right]$$

and is approximately a χ^2 distributed with m-p degrees of freedom. To significantly fit the data well, the value of the deviance (D) should be small for the model.

The parameter estimates in the chosen "best" fitted model are the maximum-likelihood estimates, but the estimation of the variance-covariance matrix of the parameter estimates leads to pseudo-likelihood. On the other hand, to measure the precision of the estimated counts in the ith small area unit, the variance of the predicted values is computed as

$$V\left(\hat{Y}_i^P\right) = \left(\hat{Y}_i^P\right)^2 X_i V X_i^T,$$

where $\hat{Y}_i^P$ is assumed to be unbiased and V is the variance-covariance matrix for $\hat{\beta}$. Additionally, the coefficient of variation, which measures the reliability of the predicted counts is computed as

$$CV\left(\hat{Y}_i^P\right) = \frac{\sqrt{V\left(\hat{Y}_i^P\right)}}{\hat{Y}_i^P} \times 100\%.$$

Moreover, a 95% confidence interval (C.I.) of the predicted values is constructed using the expression $C.I. = \hat{Y}_i^P \mp 1.96\sqrt{V\left(\hat{Y}_i^P\right)}.$

As an illustration, consider estimating the provincial-level proportion of underweight children aged 0–5 years, where the estimator to be used is defined as $\hat{P}_i^P = \frac{\hat{Y}_i^P}{N_i}$, where $\hat{Y}_i^P$ is the predicted count of underweight children aged 0–5 years residing in the ith province using the Poisson regression model and N_i is the population count of children aged 0–5 years in the ith province.

Initially, we must obtain the provincial direct estimates of the number of underweight children aged 0–5 years, which will serve as the dependent variable in the model. We can source this variable from a nutrition survey, and we can obtain the population counts from the most recent census data.

Employing Poisson regression estimation requires some preliminary steps, like setting the working directory and installing some R packages. The required R packages are **MASS**, **readxl**, **car**, **rsq**, and **writexl**. See Appendix 1 for a description of these packages.

```
install.packages(c("car", "MASS", "readxl", "rsq", "writexl"), dependencies = TRUE)

library(car)
library(MASS)
library(readxl)
library(rsq)
library(writexl)
```

Step 1: Identify the dependent variable and possible predictors or independent variables, similar to the first step in regression-synthetic estimation. In the Poisson regression model, the log of direct estimates of the number of underweight children aged 0–5 years in the ith province serves as the dependent variable. The explanatory variables are selected from the variables in the census, a list of establishments, and administrative-based health data sets at the provincial level.

Step 2: Specify the functional form. The log linear regression model must be fitted with the log of the direct estimates of the count as the dependent variable:

$$\log\left(\hat{Y}_i^P\right) = \beta_0 + \beta_1 X_{i1} + \dots + \beta_p X_{ip} + u_i, \qquad i = 1, 2, \dots, m. \tag{4.24}$$

Step 3: Organize the data set. We use the data set with filename **uwpsdata.xlsx**, which can be activated in the working directory through the following command:

```
uwpsdata <- read_excel("uwpsdata.xlsx")
attach(uwpsdata)
```

Appendix 2 describes this data set. Similarly, we can view the data using the command

```
View(uwpsdata)
```

Step 4: Identify the appropriate modeling estimation procedure. Because the model to be fitted is log linear, the maximum likelihood estimation procedure is appropriate for producing robust standard errors.

Step 5: Fit a Poisson regression model (Step 2), using the estimation procedure identified in Step 4. Because the auxiliary variables correlate significantly with the direct estimates as the predictors, the following commands could produce the necessary outputs:

```
poismodel <- glm(totuw ~ pagri + pperkids, data =uwpsdata, family =  poisson())
summary(poismodel)
```

Step 6: Perform a goodness of fit test to determine whether the model fits the data for the overall model. The residual deviance can be used to test the goodness of fit of the fitted Poisson regression model.

```
with(poismodel, cbind(res.deviance = deviance, df = df.residual, p =
        pchisq(deviance, df.residual, lower.tail = FALSE)))
```

Note that a p-value less than or equal to 0.05 implies that the model does not fit the data. The goodness of fit chi-squared test should not be statistically significant to conclude that the model fits the data.

Step 7: From the "best" fitted model, generate the predicted counts as well as the corresponding standard errors of the predicted values.

```
uwpscount <- predict(poismodel, uwpsdata, level = 0, type = "response",
        se.fit = TRUE)
pscount <- uwpscount$fit
pscountse <- uwpscount$se.fit
```

We can view the predicted values and the values of the created variables by just calling the variable names (see Step 3).

Step 8: After generating the provincial estimates of the proportion of underweight children aged 0–5 years and the estimates' corresponding standard error, compute the coefficient of variation and confidence intervals of the estimates to assess the properties of the estimates.

```
uwpoiprop <- pscount/prpopcount0to5
var <- (pscountse^2) / (prpopcount0to5^2)
se <- sqrt(var)
cv <- (se/uwpoiprop)*100
ll <- uwpoiprop - (1.96*se)
ul <- uwpoiprop + (1.96*se)
```

The results are generated and relevant statistics are placed in an Excel spreadsheet using the **.xlsx** format.

```
uwpdata <- cbind(uwpsdata[-c(5:121)],pscount, pscountse, uwpoiprop, var,
        se, cv, ll, ul)
write_xlsx(uwpdata, "uwpois.xlsx")
```

The generated estimates per province (**uwpoiprop**) as well as their corresponding variance (**var**), standard error (**se**), coefficient of variation (**cv**), and lower (**ll**) and upper limits (**ul**) can be accessed in the Excel file **uwpois.xlsx** located in the working directory. The description of this data set is available in Appendix 2.

4.3.4 Logistic Regression Estimation

In some cases, a discrete response variable takes only two possible values (i.e., 1 and 0). For example, the response variable takes one of only two possible values representing "success" ($y = 1$ or presence of an attribute of interest) and "failure" ($y = 0$ or absence of an attribute of interest). For such cases, the logistic regression model is appropriate, where a categorical dependent variable Y is regressed on a set of independent variables represented by $X_1, X_2, \ldots, X_n$.

Logistic regression resembles Poisson regression, but the regression estimates the log odds of the event of interest given a set of independent variables rather than estimating the log of the expected counts of the variable of interest. In other words, the function of a set of independent variables is used to predict a logit transformation of the dependent variable, $\ln\left(\dfrac{p_i}{1 - p_i}\right)$, where p_i is the probability of observing "success."

Moreover, it is assumed that responses $Y_1, Y_2, \ldots, Y_i$ are independent Bernoulli random variables[12] with probability p_i.

Application of logistic regression model in SAE implies that the estimated probability of occurrence of an event in the ith small area unit, $\hat{p}_i$, is related to the set of predictors (X) through the following expression:

$$\ln\left(\frac{\hat{p}_i}{1 - \hat{p}_i}\right) = X_i^T \hat{\beta} + u_i \qquad i = 1, 2, \ldots m, \tag{4.25}$$

where X_i^T is a $1 \times k$ vector of auxiliary count data about the ith small area unit;

$\hat{\beta}$ is the logistic regression estimator of a $k \times 1$ vector of regression parameters, denoted by β; and

μ_i is a vector of independent random errors, which are distributed with mean 0 and variance-covariance matrix expressed as $\sigma^2 I$.

The predicted probability values can then be expressed as $\hat{p}_i = \dfrac{e^{X_i^T \hat{\beta}}}{1 + e^{X_i^T \hat{\beta}}}$, which

represents the probability that the ith small area possesses the attribute of interest or the proportion of the units in the ith small area possessing the attribute of interest. A measure of the overall fit of the logistic model to the data set is the deviance statistic D, which can be computed as

$$D = 2\sum_{i=1}^{m}\left[w_i\left(y_i \ln\left(\frac{y_i}{\hat{p}_i}\right) + (1 - y_i)\ln\left(\frac{1 - y_i}{1 - \hat{p}_i}\right)\right)\right], \tag{4.26}$$

where D is approximately an χ^2 distributed with $m\text{-}p$ degrees of freedom. To significantly fit the data well, the value of the deviance should be small for the model. Meanwhile, in measuring the precision of the predicted probabilities or proportions for the ith small area unit, the variance of the predicted values is given by $V(\hat{p}_i) = X_i V X_i^T$, where V is the estimated variance-covariance matrix of the estimated coefficients $\hat{\beta}$,

---

[12] A Bernoulli random variable is the simplest kind of random variable, which can take on two values (i.e., 1 and 0). For example in an experiment, it takes a value of 1 with probability p if it resulted in success and a value of 0 otherwise (https://web.stanford.edu/class/archive/cs/cs109/cs109.1178/lectureHandouts/070-bernoulli-binomial.pdf).

which is equal to the inverse of the information matrix $I(\hat{\boldsymbol{\beta}})$. Using this measure of precision, the coefficient of variation of the predicted probabilities is computed as $CV(\hat{p}_i) = \dfrac{\sqrt{V(\hat{p}_i)}}{(\hat{p}_i)} \times 100\%$. A 95% C.I. of the predicted probabilities is constructed using the equation $C.I. = \hat{p}_i \mp 1.96\sqrt{V(\hat{p}_i)}$.

For illustration, consider again estimating the provincial level proportion of underweight children aged 0–5 years, where the estimator to be used is defined as $\hat{P}_i^P = \dfrac{\hat{Y}_i^P}{N_i}$ with $\hat{Y}_i^P$ as the predicted count of underweight children aged 0–5 years residing in the ith province using the Poisson regression model, and N_i is the population count of children aged 0–5 years in the ith province. These estimates can be used to classify whether a province is nutritionally depressed. For this purpose, we used the definition given by World Health Organization (WHO) in 1995.

According to WHO, a proportion greater than or equal to 30% implies a very high prevalence of underweight children aged 0–5 years (i.e., an alarming number of children aged 0–5 years in the province suffer from severe underweight). Thus, a province having a greater than or equal to 30% proportion of underweight children aged 0–5 years can be categorized as nutritionally depressed.

In **Step 1** of the modeling process, variable of interest Y_i, which is defined as the nutritional status of the ith province, is a binary variable taking the value 1 if the province is nutritionally depressed and 0, otherwise. This is mathematically defined as $Y_i = \begin{cases} 1 & \text{if } \hat{P}_i^P \geq 0.30 \\ 0 & \text{if } \hat{P}_i^P < 0.30 \end{cases}$. The possible predictors are characteristics of the ith province.

In **Step 2**, we specified the functional form to use in modeling. With a response variable that is a binary variable, a logistic regression estimation method is appropriate. An appropriate model of a logistic regression model is expressed as

$$\text{logit}\begin{pmatrix} \text{probability that the } i^{th} \text{ province} \\ \text{is nutritionally depressed} \end{pmatrix} = \ln\begin{pmatrix} \text{probability that the } i^{th} \text{ province} \\ \text{is nutritionally depressed} \\ \hline \text{probability that the } i^{th} \text{ province} \\ \text{is not nutritionally depressed} \end{pmatrix}$$

$$\ln\left(\frac{\hat{p}_i}{1-\hat{p}_i}\right) = \beta_0 + \beta_1 X_1 + ... + \beta_{k1} X_k + u \tag{4.27}$$

$$\ln\left(\frac{\hat{p}_i}{1-\hat{p}_i}\right) = X_i^T \hat{\boldsymbol{\beta}} + u_i \qquad\qquad i = 1,2,...m$$

In **Step 3**, we organized the data set to be used. For this illustration, the explanatory variables are selected from the variables in the census of population, list of establishments, and administrative-based health data sets at the provincial level. These explanatory variables, together with the variable on nutritional status of the provinces (**ndp**), which serves as the dependent variable are available in the data set ***uwlogdata.xlsx***. See Appendix 2 for a description of this data set.

To employ logit regression estimation, we need to do preliminary steps, such as setting the working directory and installing some R packages. The required R packages are ***readxl***, ***car***, ***rsq***, ***caret***, ***InformationValue*** and ***writexl***. Appendix 1 describes these packages.

```
install.packages(c("car", "caret", "InformationValue", "readxl", "rsq", "writexl"), dependencies = TRUE)

library(car)
library(caret)
library(InformationValue)
library(readxl)
library(rsq)
library(writexl)

uwlogdata <- read_excel("uwlogdata.xlsx")
```

In Step 4, we identified the appropriate modeling estimation procedure. Since the model to be fitted is log linear, the maximum likelihood estimation procedure is appropriate to use to produce robust standard errors.

In Step 5, we fitted a logistic regression model with the auxiliary variables as the predictors using the **logmodel** command. Other commands (e.g., **rsq.kl** and **vif**) can produce the needed statistics to check the assumptions of the model. Likewise, we need to check whether the model fits the data by performing a goodness of fit test for the overall model. We can use the residual deviance to test the goodness of fit of the fitted logistic regression model. The statistics generated by these commands are needed to perform residual analysis in **Step 6**.

```
logmodel <- glm(ndp ~ pagri + pwomathsed, data=uwlogdata, family =
    binomial())
summary(logmodel)
rsq.kl(logmodel)
vif(logmodel)
with(logmodel, cbind(res.deviance = deviance, df = df.residual, p =
    pchisq(deviance, df.residual, lower.tail = FALSE)))
```

In Step 7, we generated the predicted probabilities from the "best" fitted model, as well as the corresponding standard error of the predicted probabilities.

```
uwlogpred <- predict(logmodel, uwlogdata, level = 0, type = "response", se.fit = TRUE)
uwpreprob <- uwlogpred$fit
uwpreprobse <- uwlogpred$se.fit
```

Step 8 used the generated standard errors to assess the statistical properties of the estimates. We can conduct further analysis to check the "goodness" of the procedure (i.e., identify the classification of each of the province, using the predicted probabilities from the "best" fitted model, and generating the misclassification rate, sensitivity, and specificity of the model as additional model diagnostics.

```
threshold <- optimalCutoff(uwlogdata$ndp, uwpreprob)[1]
threshold
prstat <- ifelse(uwpreprob > threshold, 1, 0)
actstat <- logmodel$y
conf_matrix <- table(prstat, actstat)
conf_matrix
misClassError(actstat, prstat, threshold)
sensitivity(actstat, prstat, threshold)
specificity(actstat, prstat, threshold)
cv <- uwpreprobse/uwpreprob
ll <- uwpreprob - (1.96*uwpreprobse)
ul <- uwpreprob + (1.96*uwpreprobse)
```

We can export the results generated in **.xlsx** format using the following command:

```
uwstatdata <- cbind(uwlogdata[-c(3:123)],uwpreprob, prstat, uwpreprobse,
  cv, ll, ul)
write_xlsx(uwstatdata, "uwlog.xlsx")
```

The predicted probabilities per province (**uwpreprob**) and the predicted classification of the province (**prstat**), standard error (**uwpreprobse**), coefficient of variation (**cv**), and lower (**ll**) and upper limits (**ul**) of the predicted probabilities can now be accessed in the Excel file **uwlog.xlsx** located in the working directory. See Appendix 2 for a description of this data set.

Figure 4.2 shows the major processes in undertaking SAE while Table 4.3 summarizes the different SAE methodologies.

Figure 4.2: Small Area Estimation Process

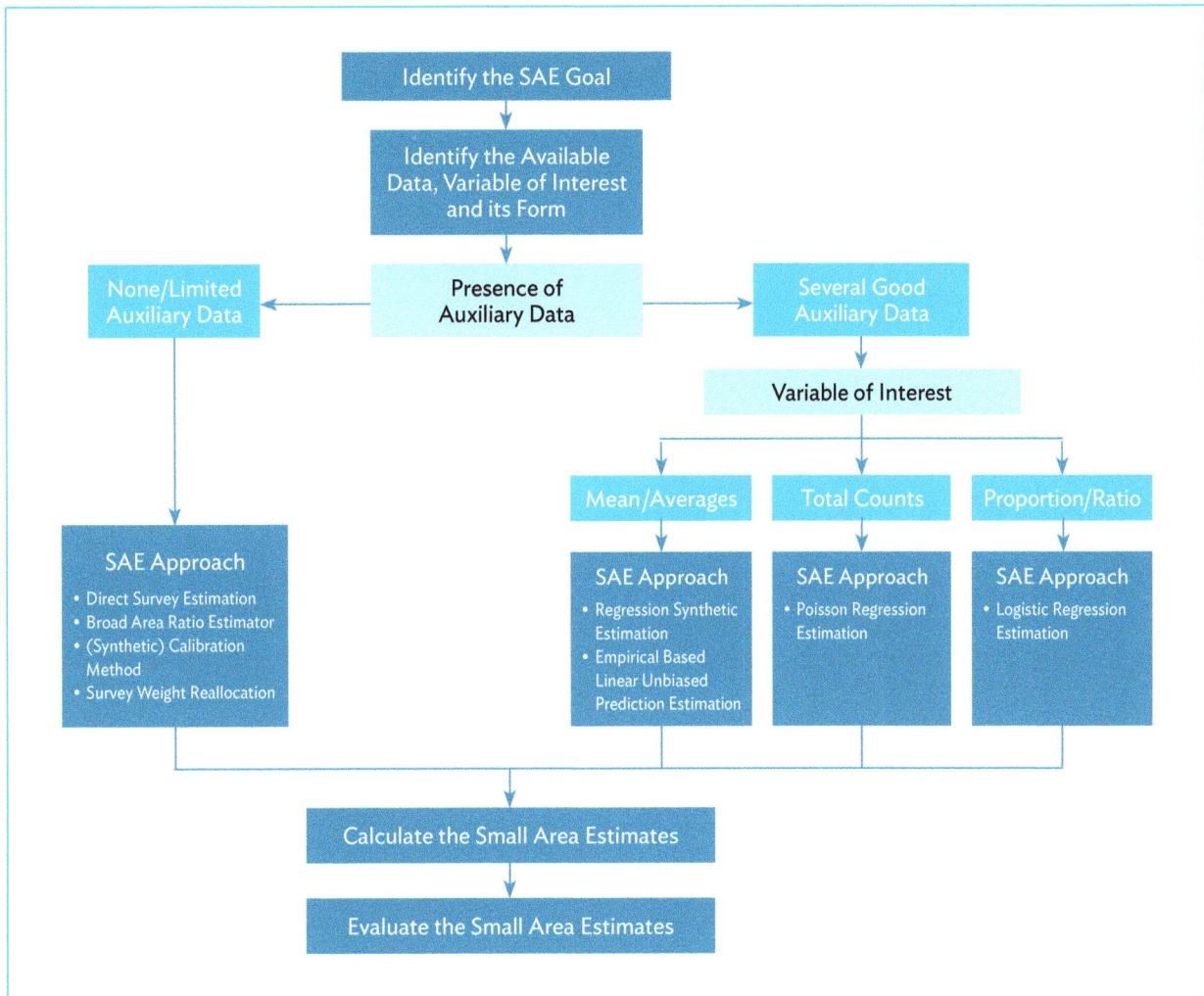

```
                    Identify the SAE Goal

              Identify the Available
              Data, Variable of Interest
              and its Form

None/Limited          Presence of            Several Good
Auxiliary Data    ←   Auxiliary Data    →    Auxiliary Data

                                             Variable of Interest

                          Mean/Averages    Total Counts    Proportion/Ratio

SAE Approach          SAE Approach       SAE Approach     SAE Approach
• Direct Survey       • Regression       • Poisson        • Logistic
  Estimation            Synthetic          Regression       Regression
• Broad Area Ratio      Estimation         Estimation       Estimation
  Estimator           • Empirical Based
• (Synthetic)           Linear Unbiased
  Calibration           Prediction
  Method                Estimation
• Survey Weight
  Reallocation

              Calculate the Small Area Estimates

              Evaluate the Small Area Estimates
```

SAE = small area estimation.
Source: Australian Bureau of Statistics. 2006. A Guide to Small Area Estimation.

Table 4.3: Summary of Different Small Area Estimation Methods

SAE Method	Brief Description	Model Type	Auxiliary Data	Advantages	Disadvantages
A. Direct Survey Estimation					
	Classical estimators that are obtained by applying survey weights to the sample units in each small area	Simple small area	None	Most straightforward methodology for disaggregating an indicator that is compiled using survey data	Reliability depends on the representativeness of sample data collected
B. Small Area Estimation Using Auxiliary Information					
1. **Broad Area Ratio Estimator**	Calculated by pro-rating a broad area direct estimate by the ratio of the small area to broad area populations	Simple small area	Limited	Simple and straightforward	Major assumption that the small areas share the same characteristics as the large area to generate unbiased estimates
2. **(Synthetic) Calibration Methods**	A technique that uses sample data to estimate, at some higher level of aggregation, the variable of interest for different subclasses of the population, then scales these estimates in proportion to the subclass of incidence within the small domains of interest	Simple small area	Limited	Simple and intuitive – easy to implement because it applies to general sampling designs; method borrows information from similar small areas to increase the accuracy of the resulting estimates; also produces consistent estimates	Synthetic estimators assume that certain areas are similar and failure to satisfy this assumption can result to large bias
3. **Survey Weight Reallocation Using Auxiliary Information From Statistical Neighbors**	The principle is to artificially increase the sample size in a specific small area by including in the calculation information from sampled units from all statistical neighbors of the given small area		Limited	Sampled units from other neighboring sub-areas can be used to estimate characteristics for a sub-area, thus "synthetically increasing" the sample	Computationally intensive; potential bias that weight reallocation may induce, especially when the statistical neighbors are not homogeneous with respect to the indicator of interest

continued on next page

Table 4.3 *continued*

SAE Method	Brief Description	Model Type	Auxiliary Data	Advantages	Disadvantages
C. Small Area Estimation Using Regression-Based Models					
1. **Regression-Synthetic Estimation**	Estimate local area parameters using a multiple linear regression, assuming that the variable of interest is linearly dependent with the auxiliary variables, and applying independent variables obtained from either censuses or administrative records	Regression based	Several good auxiliary data	Models can generate efficient estimates, and sample data can validate the models. It can handle complex cases such as cross-sectional and time-series data. The estimates obtained in this method include specific measures of variability.	Stronger data requirements Needs regression knowledge to implement correct model (e.g., poisson, logistic) Complex modeling entails strong statistical skills and longer time
2. **Empirical Best Linear Unbiased Prediction Estimation**	Weighted combination of design-based estimator and regression-synthetic estimator	Regression based	Several good auxiliary data		
3. **Poisson Regression Estimation**	Model assumes that the response variable, which refers to the number of occurrences of the event of interest, has a Poisson distribution	Regression based	Several good auxiliary data		
4. **Logistic Regression Estimation**	Resembles Poisson regression, but the regression estimates the log odds of the event of interest given a set of independent variables rather than estimating the log of the expected counts of the variable of interest	Regression based	Several good auxiliary data		

CHAPTER V
VISUALIZING SMALL AREA ESTIMATES USING R

Data visualization is an increasingly popular tool for understanding enormous amount of data generated every day and translating these data into story to inform policies and programs. Visual elements (e.g., graphs, charts and maps) can simplify explanation of statistical data patterns, trends and outliers. Using these tools can effectively present SAE results. For instance, a map can visually show the geographic variation of poverty at the small area and explain where poverty is least and most concentrated.

R software can make SAE data an attribute of a vector spatial data and thus visualized the data as maps. To illustrate the visualization of small area estimates as spatial data in R, Step 1 undertakes preliminary steps, such as setting the working directory using command "setwd()," installing the needed packages using the command "install.packages()," and loading the needed packages using the command "library()". The required R packages are *sf*, *ggplot2*, and *readxl*.

```
install.packages(c("ggplot2","readxl","sf"),dependencies = TRUE)
library (ggplot2)
library (readxl)
library (sf)
```

Step 2 involves loading the data sets. We will use data from Table 4.1 (poverty_bare.xlsx) and the vector shapefile of the hypothetical province X. To load the data from Table 4.1, which is stored in an Excel file, we use the command "read_excel()." Meanwhile, to load the vector shapefiles, we use the command "st_read()" using the package **sf** to read vector shapefiles. The package sf structures spatial data, known as "spatial features," uses a language-independent standard.

```
poverty_bare <- read_excel("poverty_bare.xlsx")
prov_shp <- st_read("Province_X_bnd.shp")
```

Step 3 merges Table 4.1 data with the vector shapefile, using the "merge()" command to create a new shapefile attribute. Note that both data sets are merged by municipality, the common identifier between the two data.

```
prov_shp <- merge(prov_shp,poverty_bare,
         by.x = "mun", by.y="mun")
```

Step 4 uses the functionalities of ggplot2 to generate the population and number of poor population maps of province X. This can be done using the command "ggplot(data = <*shapefile*>)" in conjunction with the function "geom_sf(aes(fill = <*shapefile attribute*>))" to specify the shapefile attribute to be visualized.

The succeeding functions are used to improve the aesthetics of the map. Function "scale_fill_viridis_c(option = <*color map option*>, name=<*color scale title*>)" specifies the use of viridis color scales as our map fill to represent the data we are visualizing. "Option" indicates the appropriate colormap (i.e. "cividis," "inferno," "magma," "plasma," and "viridis" (default)), while "name" specifies the color scale legend title. Viridis color scales were preferred because they are designed to be easily recognizable by viewers with common forms of color blindness. Function "ggtitle()" adds the map title, and functions "theme(plot.title = element_text(hjust = 0.5))" and "theme(plot.title = element_text(face = "bold"))" center aligns and sets the map title to bold characters, respectively.

```
#generate population map

population_map <- ggplot(data = prov_shp) +
  geom_sf(aes(fill = popn_mun)) +
  scale_fill_viridis_c(option = "plasma", name="Population")+
  ggtitle("Population of Province X")+
  theme(plot.title = element_text(hjust = 0.5))+
  theme(plot.title = element_text(face = "bold"))

#generate number of poor population map

poor_population_map <- ggplot(data = prov_shp) +
  geom_sf(aes(fill = povcount_mun)) +
  scale_fill_viridis_c(option = "viridis", name="Poor Population") +
  ggtitle("Number of Poor Population in Province X")+
  theme(plot.title = element_text(hjust = 0.5))+
  theme(plot.title = element_text(face = "bold"))
```

To view the maps, we issue the variable names of the two maps into the R console.

```
> population_map
> poor_population_map
```

Should you opt to save the maps you created, you may use the command "ggsave()." In ggplot2 version 0.9.0, the file extensions recognized are bmp, eps/ps, jpeg, pdf, png, svg, tex (pictex), tiff, and wmf. The "plot" option specifies the ggplot object to save, in this case the generated map. The "height" and "weight" options specify the object dimension, and the "units" option specifies the dimension's unit of measure. The "dpi" option, short for dots per inch, specifies the plot resolution of the object to be saved. Other resolution options include "retina" (320dpi), "print" (300dpi), and "screen" (72dpi).

CHAPTER VI | CONCLUSION

Contemporary development practitioners agree that socioeconomic development goes beyond increasing people's incomes, with recent discussion converging into an agreement that it touches on multiple dimensions of development. Although minimizing income poverty remains a very important theme of a socioeconomic development agenda, such a narrow conceptualization of development ignores that income interacts with other aspects of people's living standards.

Since we embarked on various international development agendas, from the MDGs to the SDGs, many countries have witnessed an incredible journey from poverty to wider prosperity, accompanied by faster economic growth, rising life expectancy, and higher literacy rates. Notwithstanding the progress attained on these fronts, much work remains to close the gap between the rich and poor. A deeper understanding of which segments of societies are being left behind requires more granular data to allow a closer examination of trends across different population groups. In fact, the SDGs espouse the principle of "leaving no one behind" and disaggregation of select indicators by geographic location, sex, age, and occupation, among other dimensions. Availability of granular or disaggregated data will provide a solid basis for understanding progress, or lack thereof, toward various development goals and targets. While many countries in Asia and the Pacific disaggregate SDG data on several dimensions, such data often are not granular enough to provide more nuanced understanding of who lags behind.

National statistical systems understand the importance of producing disaggregated and granular data to shed more light on the profile of the persistently poor and disadvantaged. However, compiling such data requires additional resources. Given the importance of granular data to effective monitoring of the SDGs—particularly the pursuit of poverty reduction—while managing the cost of data collection, it is important that NSOs explore cost-effective methods of compiling granular data.

SAE offers an important example of a method that combines multiple data sources to provide more reliable granular data than individual data sources can produce on their own. In the case of poverty statistics, for instance, sample sizes of survey data sets used for poverty estimation are rarely large enough to generate reliable estimates for highly disaggregated analysis. This guide has introduced readers to basic SAE methods, which can be broadly classified according to the type of auxiliary data requirements and the level at which they are available. BARE and survey weight reallocation are examples of SAE techniques that do not require significant amounts of auxiliary data. On the other hand, empirical best linear unbiased prediction and other regression-based SAE methods have stronger data requirements, but they tend to facilitate more gains in terms of estimate reliability. Furthermore, the choice of a SAE technique depends on several considerations, which should be specified upfront in one's SAE implementation plan. These considerations include the main objective of conducting SAE, form of indicator or variable of interest, desired level of granularity or disaggregation, availability of data, technical resources, and communication strategy.

This guide provides practical examples of implementing different SAE techniques, particularly in the context of estimating indicators on poverty, employment, and health outcomes. It also discusses software implementation using R, giving readers the opportunity to apply the methods discussed here, using easily accessible analytical platform which anyone with internet access can readily acquire in their own analytical work or research.

We hope that this guide will help NSOs and other development practitioners, particularly those who lack background experience with SAE, (i) direct their attention to data disaggregation using a combination of direct and indirect estimation methods, (ii) establish a proper baseline and succeeding time series data of SDG indicators that will allow socioeconomic planners to develop and implement targeted policies, and (iii) ensure that the vulnerable segments of societies will not be left behind.

APPENDIXES

Appendix 1: Description of R Packages Identified and Used in the Illustrations

R Package Title	Description
car	Generates vif of the fitted general linear model
caret	Analyzes sensitivity and specificity of the logistic model
dplyr	Manipulates data sets in R
ggplot2	Creates graphics[a]
InformationValue	Analyzes sensitivity and specificity of the logistic model
leaps	Performs an exhaustive search for the best subsets of the variables in x for predicting y in linear regression
lmtest	Tests linear regression models
MASS	Fits a model
readstata13	Reads and writes data in "Stata" file format
readxl	Imports Excel files in R
rsq	Generates the R-square of the fitted general linear model
sae	Conducts empirical best linear unbiased prediction (EBLUP) procedure
sf	Standardized method for encoding spatial vector data
survey	Analyzes complex survey samples
tidyr	Tidies data
writexl	Exports data from R to Excel file

[a] Based on the book *The Grammar of Graphics*, which provides fundamentals for generating nearly all quantitative graphic shown in scientific journals, newspapers, statistical software, and data visualization structure (https://www.springer.com/gp/book/9780387245447).
Source: RStudio.

Appendix 2: Data Files Identified and Used in Illustrations

File Name	Description
countryx_demographics_01.xlsx	Contains information on seven provinces in Country X, including region code, province name, female and male population, and land area
country_demographics_02.xlsx	Contains information on another seven provinces in Country X, including region code, province name, female and male population, and land area
country_home.xlsx	Contains the number of homes for all provinces in Country X
country_poverty_rate.xlsx	Contains poverty rate in select provinces of Country X
data for weight reallocation.dta	Contains information on five provinces, including region code, province code, total expenditure, household size, sex of household head, and educational attainment of household head
eblup_finaldata.xlsx	Contains the provincial empirical best linear unbiased prediction (EBLUP) estimates of the proportion of households with income below 50% of the national median income as well as corresponding standard errors, coefficients of variation, and lower and upper limits of the confidence interval estimates
hh_survey.xlsx	Contains information on region, household size, total household expenditure, total per capita expenditure, total household income, sex of the household head, and age of the household head
hies.xlsx	Contains the poverty indicator at the household level (i.e., whether the household is poor, primary sampling unit, stratum, and weights)
hiescph.xlsx	Contains the provincial direct estimates of the proportion of households with income below 50% of the national median income generated using the income and expenditure survey data set, and provincial values of auxiliary variables from the census of population and housing
long_population.xlsx	Contains the regional population count by sex of Country X
poverty_bare.xlsx	Contains the population of each municipality in province X, poverty rate of province X, and magnitude of poor population for each municipality
Province_X_bnd.shp	Contains the shapefile of each municipality in province X
syn_reg_finaldata.xlsx	Contains provincial regression-synthetic estimates of the proportion of households with income below 50% of the national median income as well as corresponding standard errors, coefficients of variation, and lower and upper limits of the confidence interval estimates
uwlogdata.xlsx	Contains provincial nutritional status obtained using the direct estimates of the number of 0–5-year-old underweight children and provincial values of auxiliary variables from the population census, administrative-based health data set, and list of establishments
uwpois.xlsx	Contains the Poisson estimates of the provincial proportion of 0–5-year-old underweight children as well as corresponding standard errors, coefficients of variation, and lower and upper limits of the confidence interval estimates

continued on next page

Appendix 2 *continued*

File Name	Description
uwpsdata.xlsx	Contains the provincial direct estimates of the number of 0–5-year-old underweight children, generated from the nutrition survey, and provincial values of auxiliary variables from the population census; administrative-based health data; and list of establishments
uwlog.xlsx	Contains the provincial predicted probabilities of having 0–5-year-old underweight children, along with predicted classification of the province whether the province is nutritionally depressed, and corresponding standard errors, coefficients of variation, and lower and upper limits of the confidence interval estimates
wide_poverty.xlsx	Contains the regional poverty rate of Country X from 2014 to 2016

Note: Available upon request through amartinezjr@adb.org.
Source: Authors' compilation of hypothetical data and shape files.

Appendix 3: Model Building

The model-based approach to small area estimation is generally regression-based, and models used in this approach can be classified as either regression-synthetic or random effects. Regression-synthetic models use available auxiliary data to express a deterministic relationship between auxiliary variables and the target variable. The relationship between the auxiliary variables and the target variable could be established through correlation analysis.

The modeling process assumes that all systematic variability in the target variable is explained by the variability in the values of the auxiliary variables. Any remaining variability is represented as a residual and technically referred to as "random noise" or "stochastic variation." Residuals are the differences between the predicted values of the target variable using the resulting model of the process and the observed values from the data.

Incorporating a random effect into the model results in a different kind of model, which treats the intercept term as fixed constants. Additionally, a random component measures the random effect. This kind of model considers variability among small areas. Although the two kinds of models are different, the framework used in the process is almost the same.

1.   The Modeling Framework

In the model-based approach, a functional relationship is formulated between the variable of interest, or indicator, and the auxiliary variables, which serve as predictors. The function could be either linear or nonlinear, and the functional form dictates the estimation procedure to use in fitting the data to the identified functional form. The modeling process can be done at the area level or the unit level. The difference lies on the available data that will be used in the modeling process:

* Aggregate or area level models that relate the small area means to area-specific auxiliary variables.[1]
* Unit level models that relate the unit values of the variable of interest to unit-specific auxiliary variables.[2]

Aggregate models are used more commonly, because unit-level data are seldom available. They generally adhere to the following steps:

Step 1: Identify the variable of interest (i.e., dependent variable) and possible predictors (i.e., independent variables).
Step 2: Specify the functional form.
Step 3: Organize the data.
Step 4: Choose the appropriate modeling estimation procedure.
Step 5: Using the modeling estimation procedure identified in Step 4, fit the functional form identified in Step 2 and determine the "best" fitted model.

---

[1]   These models are also called Fay and Herriot models. Such models are essential if unit (element) level data are not available.
[2]   These models were first introduced by Battese, et al. in 1988.

Step 6: Perform residual analysis to verify that the assumptions of the model (functional form) are satisfied. If the assumptions are satisfied, proceed to Step 7. Otherwise, perform remedial measures to satisfy assumptions of the model and return to Step 5.

Step 7: Use the model to generate the small area estimates.

Step 8: Assess the statistical properties of the estimates. If the estimates fail the assessment, go back to Step 2. Otherwise, the results of Step 7 are the final small area estimates.

In Step 1, the variable of interest or the indicator to be estimated is the dependent variable. Likewise, identify auxiliary variables as predictors. Correlation analysis is a statistical technique that could be used to identify auxiliary variables (see Chapter IV, Section 4.3). Results of related previous studies and opinions of relevant subject matter specialists could be sources of information to identify auxiliary variables.

After identifying the variables involved in the modeling process, the next step is to identify the functional form that will appropriately depict the relationship among the variables. The assumptions or conditions that need to be satisfied in order to use the functional form should be verified using the sample data to be used in the modeling process. Thus, it is very important to have an organized data set before starting the modeling process. Note that the level at which the modeling is to be done could be decided based on the available data (i.e., with the organized data set, one can now decide whether to do area- or unit-level modeling).

With the identified variables, functional form, and organized data, we can identify the estimation procedure. Available estimation procedures include least squares, maximum likelihood, and Bayesian estimation. The least squares estimation procedure is the most common procedure because it has the least requirements to be satisfied unlike the other two methods. In the last two estimation procedures, users must satisfy the distributional assumptions conceptually according to the data. Checking this is important because nonsatisfaction of the assumptions leads to invalid results.

In Step 5, the "best" fitted model is the targeted output. Several procedures can be used to obtain the "best" model. "Best" means that the model is not only adequate or fitted to the data, but also statistically significant, with all of its regression coefficients also being statistically significant at an acceptable significance level. The existing procedures include forward selection, backward elimination and stepwise regression. More detailed description of these procedures is given in next subsection.

Residual analysis is a way to verify whether the assumptions of the model being fitted are satisfied empirically. This is done in Step 6. With the residuals as estimates of the model error, statistical tests could be conducted to verify the satisfaction of assumptions.

After obtaining the "best" model, it can be used to generate the small area estimates. This is done in Step 7. The generated estimates in Step 7 must be assessed, as mentioned in Step 8. Chapter II discusses how one can evaluate the generated estimates.

Note that the modeling process is repetitive in nature and would only end if one is already satisfied with the final estimates as the output of the process.

2. Procedures in Finding the "Best" Model

There are several procedures that can be used to find the "best" model. As described earlier, the "best" model is the one that passes model evaluation in terms of satisfaction of assumptions of the model and adequacy or fitness of the model to the data set. The "best" model must also be statistically significant with all of its regression coefficients. The signs of the regression coefficients of the "best model" could be logically explained such that it follows some theories or concepts in the subject matter. More importantly, users must follow the principle of parsimony[3] when choosing the "best" model to ensure its cost-efficiency when generating the estimates.

There are several procedures to find the "best" model, but most of them are already given as option in statistical software. Hence, to invoke a procedure, one simply identifies it as an option for estimation. Since each procedure has advantages and disadvantages, users must first identify which procedure to use so that it can be invoked in the modeling process. The choice of procedure will depend on factors like level of accuracy, economy of effort, and availability of the computing tool or software. Three of the most commonly used procedures are provided below.

(a) Forward Selection Procedure

In this procedure, a candidate predictor enters the model one at a time. The simple or partial correlation coefficient is usually used to choose which predictor enters. The significance of the model is checked every time a new predictor enters a model. The process stops when the resulting model becomes insignificant.

This is the most computationally efficient procedure. However, it fails to consider the effect of a newly entered predictor on the variables already in the model. Thus, it builds the model by adding predictors one at a time and stopping when the most recently entered predictor does not contribute significantly to the model.

(b) Backward Elimination Procedure

The opposite of forward selection procedure is backward elimination procedure, which starts with a full model and then removes predictors from the model one at a time. The partial contribution of the predictor, through the partial F-statistics,[4] to the variability of the model is used as basis for choosing which predictor to remove. The significance of the model is checked every time a predictor is removed, and the process stops when the contribution of all predictors is significant.

This procedure is said to produce the "best" model with high probability. However, it irrevocably removes predictors at an early stage simply because of their correlation to other predictors. Also, if there are too many possible predictors, the full model might not be attainable.

---

[3] The principle of parsimony means that models should include relatively few predictors.
[4] The partial F test is used to verify whether the additional variables provide sufficient explanatory power to justify their inclusion in the model (https://www.coursehero.com/file/p4sbnnq/The-partial-F-test-is-used-to-determine-whether-the-extra-variables-provide/).

(c)   Stepwise Regression Procedure

The stepwise regression procedure was developed by combining the good features of the forward selection procedure and the backward elimination procedure. Stepwise regression uses correlation coefficients and a partial contribution by the predictor to the variability of the model as bases for the entry and removal of the predictors. Hence, the basis of entry and removal of the predictors is the basis used by both procedures described earlier. Consequently, stepwise regression is more computationally intensive. However, its popularity has made it the default option in most existing statistical software.

3.   Testing Assumptions of a Model

Models to be fitted have certain assumptions or conditions that the data set must satisfy to get a good fit of the model. Nonsatisfaction of these assumptions may lead to invalid results. Thus, it is important to know what these assumptions are and which statistical tests could be used to check whether these assumptions have been satisfied. Here, the case of fitting a linear model will illustrate our discussion of some statistical tests.

A linear model has the following assumptions:

- The relationship between the variable of interest and predictors is linear so that the function used to express the relationship depicts a line and the mathematical expression for a linear model is given by

$$y_i = \beta_0 + \beta_j x_{ij} + v_i, i = 1,2,...n; j = 1,2,...p,$$

- where y_i is the observed value of the variable of interest in the ith small area, x_{ij} is the observed value of the jth predictor in the ith small area, v_i is the error term associated in the ith small area, and β's are the regression coefficients. This is also known as the assumption of linearity.
- The predictors are uncorrelated or there is no multicollinearity among the predictors.
- The mean of the error term is equal to 0, that is, $E[v_i] = 0$ for all i.
- The variance of the error term is constant, that is, $Var[v_i] = \sigma^2$, a constant for all i. This is the assumption of homoscedasticity.
- There is no autocorrelation of the error term, that is, $Cov[v_i v_j] = 0$ for $i \neq j$.

In addition to these assumptions, there is an assumption of normality of the error term, specifically when statistical inference is to be employed in the analysis. The assumption of normality states that the error term is normally distributed with mean 0 and variance, σ². In symbols, this is $v_i \sim N(0,\sigma^2)$. The assumption of normality is necessary when the statistical significance test is to be conducted on the regression coefficients and the model itself.

The assumption of linearity implies that apart from the random error, the observations on the variable of interest and one predictor, when plotted in the X-Y plane, will be scattered about a straight line. Graphically, the assumption of linearity can easily be verified. In the regression context, linearity refers to the manner in which the parameters enter the equation and not necessarily to the relationship between X and Y. Some models that satisfy the assumption of linearity include

- $y_i = \beta_0 + \beta_j e^{x_{ij}} + v_i, i = 1,2,...n; j = 1,2,...p$,

- $y_i = \beta_0 + \beta_j \left(\dfrac{1}{x_{ij}}\right) + v_i, i = 1,2,...n; j = 1,2,...p$, and

- $y_i = \beta_0 + \beta_j \ln x_{ij} + v_i, i = 1,2,...n; j = 1,2,...p$.

Multicollinearity is an excessive correlation among predictors. This condition prevents identification of an optimal set of explanatory variables. The variance inflation factor (VIF) is usually computed as an indicator of the presence of multicollinearity. Broadly, VIF exceeding 4 warrants investigation, while VIF exceeding 10 signals serious multicollinearity and requires action to correct the problem. An easy way to correct this problem is to drop one of the correlated predictors. Most statistical software can generate the value of VIF for a given model by invoking a command or an option.

The other assumptions are about the error term. An estimate of the error term is the residual $\hat{e}_i$ which is used to test the assumptions. Thus, testing assumptions about the error term is commonly called residual analysis. The assumption of zero mean of the error term is tested by getting the mean of the residuals and using a two-tailed t-test on one population mean to test whether the assumption of zero mean is being satisfied. Rejection of the null hypothesis on the mean equal to zero implies a violation of the assumption.

On the other hand, the assumption of homoscedasticity could be tested using the Breusch-Pagan test where the null hypothesis is that the variances is equal to a constant value. The Breusch-Pagan test requires regressing $\left(\dfrac{\hat{e}_i^2}{\hat{e}'\hat{e}/n}\right)$ on a constant and a set of predictors **x**, after which users must obtain sum of squares due to the regression of the fitted line (SSReg). Use this to compute the test statistic given as 0.5SSReg, which follows a chi-square distribution with p degrees of freedom, where p is the number of predictors in **x**. Large test statistic value leads to rejection of the null hypothesis.

The Durbin-Watson test for autocorrelation is used to test the assumption of non-autocorrelation of the error terms. The Durbin-Watson test statistic is computed using the residuals, and can be invoked as an option or command in most statistical software. Also, the residuals are used to test the assumption of normality. Wilk-Shapiro test is usually used for this purpose.

If all the assumptions of the model are satisfied, then it indicates that the model is fitted to the data set. In a case where some assumptions are not satisfied, there are remedies that can be done or other type of models could be fitted. But note that the other models have also assumptions to satisfy. For example, a Poisson regression model assumes that the variable of interest is a count data and follows the Poisson probability distribution, which has a mean equal to its variance. These assumptions must be satisfied to get a good fit of the model.

REFERENCES

Abitona, L.P.D. 2011. *Provincial Level Estimation of the Proportion of Vitamin A Deficient Children Aged 6 Months to 5 Years in the Philippines.* Unpublished Master's Thesis, University of the Philippines, Los Baños.

Albacea, Z. 1999. *Small Area Estimation of Poverty Incidence in the Philippines.* Unpublished PhD Dissertation, University of the Philippines, Los Baños.

_____ and A. Pacificador. 2003. *Targeting the Poor in the Philippines.* Research Project under the ADB Technical Assistance 3566: Improving Poverty Monitoring Surveys implemented by the National Statistics Office. Manila, National Statistics Office and Asian Development Bank.

_____.2006. *Small Area Estimation of Poverty Statistics.* Development Fund/Diamond Jubilee Professorial Chair, University of the Philippines, Los Baños.

Alcanices, M.L. 2013. *Municipal and City Level Estimation of the Total Number of Poor Households in CALABARZON and MIMAROPA Regions in the Philippines.* Unpublished Undergraduate Special Problem, Institute of Statistics. University of the Philippines, Los Baños.

Amar, R.I.Z.G. 2007. *Barangay Level Estimation of the Proportion of Underweight Filipino Children Aged 0 to 5 Years.* Unpublished Master's Thesis. University of the Philippines, Los Baños.

Amiscosa, M.F.L. 2010. *Municipal and City Level Estimation of the Number of Wasted Children Age 0-5 years old in CALABARZON.* Unpublished Undergraduate Special Problem, Institute of Statistics. University of the Philippines, Los Baños.

Aracid, S.B. 2014. *Indirect Estimates of the City and Municipality Level Counts of Underweight Children Aged 0-5 Years in MIMAROPA Region.* Unpublished Undergraduate Special Problem, Institute of Statistics. University of the Philippines, Los Baños.

Arlan, R.L. 2016. *Small Area Estimation of the City and Municipal Level Proportion of 0-5-Year-Old Underweight Children in the Philippines.* Unpublished Master's Thesis, University of the Philippines, Los Baños.

Australian Bureau of Statistics. 2006. *A Guide to Small Area Estimation-Version 1.1.* Internal ABS document.

Battese, G., Harter, R. , and Fuller, W. 1988. An error-components model for prediction of county crop areas using survey and satellite data. *Journal of the American Statistical Association.* 83(401), 28–36.

Beresovsky, V., Burt, C.W., Parsons, V., and N. Schenker. 2010. *Application of Small Area Estimation Methods to Emergency Department Data from the National Hospital Ambulatory Medical Care Survey.* Paper presented at Joint Statistical Meetings – Vancouver, British Columbia. 31 July–5 August 2010.

Bernasol, A.M.R. 2013. *Municipal and City Level Estimation of the Total Number of Poor Households in Western and Central Visayas Regions in the Philippines.* Unpublished Undergraduate Special Problem, Institute of Statistics. University of the Philippines, Los Baños.

Borromeo, M.C.B. 2011. *Estimation of the Total Number of Underemployed Filipinos in the Provinces, Selected Cities, and a Municipality in NCR.* Unpublished Undergraduate Special Problem, Institute of Statistics. University of the Philippines, Los Baños.

Bulan, J. 2011. *Municipal and City Level Estimation of the Total Number of Poor Households in Region II.* Unpublished Undergraduate Special Problem, Institute of Statistics. University of the Philippines, Los Baños.

Cameron, A.C. and P.K. Trivedi. 2009. *Microeconomics Using Stata.* College Station, TX: Stata Press.

Caisido, D.R. 2013. *Municipal and City Level Estimation of Total Number of Poor Households in Southern and Central Mindanao.* Unpublished Undergraduate Special Problem, Institute of Statistics. University of the Philippines, Los Baños.

Castillo, E., W. Molano, and Z. Albacea. 2007. *Estimating the Proportion of Stunted 0-5-Year-Old Children at the Provincial Level in the Philippines.* Paper presented at the 10th National Convention on Statistics (NCS). 1–2 October, 2007, Shangri-La Hotel, Mandaluyong City.

Chien, L-C., Lin, G., Li, X., and Zhang, X. 2018. Disparity of Imputed Data from Small Area Estimate Approaches – A Case Study on Diabetes Prevalence at the County Level in the U.S. *Data Science Journal.* 17:8, pp. 1–11.

Cochran, W. 1977. *Sampling Techniques,* 3rd Edition. John Wiley & Sons.

Cosico, A. B. G. 2007. *Estimation of Provincial Food Poverty Incidence of Households in Agriculture and Fisheries Sector in the Philippines.* Unpublished Graduate Thesis, University of the Philippines, Los Baños.

The Comprehensive R Archive Network. 2019. Package 'tidyverse'. https://cran.r-project.org/web/packages/tidyverse/tidyverse.pdf.

De Guzman, C.V. 2013. Municipal and City Level Estimation of the Total Number of Poor Household in Eastern Visayas and Cordillera Administrative Region. Unpublished Undergraduate Special Problem, Institute of Statistics. University of the Philippines, Los Baños.

De los Reyes, J.N.R. 2015. *Municipal and City Level Estimation of the Total Number of Employed Persons by Major Industry Group in Bicol Region.* Unpublished Undergraduate Special Problem, Institute of Statistics. University of the Philippines, Los Baños.

Doctolero, P.G. 2015. *Municipal and City Level Estimation of the Total Number of Employed Persons by Highest Educational Attainment in CALABARZON.* Unpublished Undergraduate Special Problem, Institute of Statistics. University of the Philippines, Los Baños.

Elazar, D. and L. Conn. 2004. *Small Area Estimation of Disability in Australia*. Research Paper presented at the Australian Statistical Conference. 11–16 July 2004, Cairns, Australia.

Elbers, C., Lanjouw, J., and P. Lanjouw. 2003. Micro-Level Estimation of Poverty and Inequality. *Econometrica*. 71(1): 355–364.

Eurostat. 2014. *Handbook on Methodology of Modern Business Statistics*. https://ec.europa.eu/eurostat/cros/content/composite-estimators-small-area-estimation-method_en.

Fay, R. and R. Herriot. 1979. Estimates of Income for Small Places: An Application of James-Stein Procedures to Census Data. *Journal of the American Statistical Association*. 74(366a), 269–277.

Ghosh, M. and J.N.K. Rao. 1994. Small Area Estimation: An Appraisal. *Statistical Science*. 9:1:55-93.

Gliponeo, L.A.S. 2017. *Sub-national Level Estimation of the Proportion of Households Who Think That There is a Serious Drug Abuse Problem in Their Community*. Unpublished Undergraduate Special Problem, Institute of Statistics. University of the Philippines, Los Baños.

Jean, N., Burke, M., Xie, M., Davis, W. Matthew, Lobell, D.B. and E. Stefano. 2016. Combining Satellite Imagery and Machine Learning to Predict Poverty. *Science*. 353(6301). pp. 790–794.

Jitsuchon, S. and K. Richter. 2007. Chapter 13 Thailand's Poverty Maps: From Construction to Application. *Thailand Northeast Economic Development Report*.

Julongbayan, L.L. 2017. *Sub-national Level Estimation of the Proportion of Households with Members Who Are Working Children Aged 5 to 17 Years*. Unpublished Undergraduate Special Problem, Institute of Statistics. University of the Philippines, Los Baños.

Lauan, M.L.B. 2010. *Municipal and City Level Estimation of the Number of Unemployed Persons in Cagayan Valley*. Unpublished Undergraduate Special Problem, Institute of Statistics. University of the Philippines, Los Baños.

Li, W., Kelsey, J.L., and Z. Zhang. 2009. Small Area Estimation and Prioritizing Communities for Obesity Control in Massachusetts. *American Journal of Public Health Income*. 99(3): 511–519.

Malec, D. 2005. Small Area Estimation from the America Community Survey Using a Hierarchical Logistic Model of Persons and Housing Units. *Journal of Statistics*. 21(3): 411–432.

McRoberts, R.E. 2010. Probability-and Model-based Approaches to Inference for Proportion Forest Using Satellite Imagery as Ancillary Data. *Remote Sensing of the Environment*. 114: 1017–1025.

Molina, I., and Y. Marhuenda. 2015. sae: An R package for small area estimation. *The R Journal*. 7(1), 81–98.

National Statistical Coordination Board. 2005. *Estimation of Local Poverty in the Philippines*. Manila.

Nuestro, I.D.P. 2014. *Municipal and City Level Estimation of the Total Number of Maternal Deaths in MIMAROPA.* Unpublished Undergraduate Special Problem, Institute of Statistics. University of the Philippines, Los Baños.

Prasad, N. N. and J.N.K. Rao. 1990. The Estimation of the Mean Squared Error of Small Area Estimators. *Journal of the American Statistical Association,* 85(409), 163–171.

Philippine Statistics Authority. 2016. *2012 Municipal and City Level Poverty Estimates.* Manila

_____ . 2013. *2006 and 2009 Municipal and City Level Poverty Estimates.* Manila.

Purcell, N.J. and L. Kish. 1979. *Estimation for Small Domains.* Biometrics. 35 48:3-18.

Rao, J.N.K. 2003. *Small Area Estimation.* Wiley Series in Survey Methodology.

Relente, C.E.N. 2010. *Municipal and City Level Estimation of the Number of Underweight 0-5-Year-Old Children in Bicol Region.* Unpublished Undergraduate Special Problem, Institute of Statistics. University of the Philippines, Los Baños.

Sangaroon, B., Kaew-Amdee, T., and B. Khananurak. 2019. *Presentation on Small Area Estimation Method and Big Data.* International Workshop on Data Disaggregation for the SDGs. Bangkok, Thailand.

Serrao, S. 2017. Presentation on SDG Data Compilation: Overview of Country Practices Related to Data Disaggregation in Asia and the Pacific.

Schirm, A. and A. Zaslavsky. 1997. Reweighting Households to Develop Microsimulation Estimates for States. Proceedings of the Survey Research Methods Section. American Statistical Association.

Schmid, T., Burckschen, F., Salvati, N. and T. Zbiranski. 2017. Constructing Socio-Demographic Indicators for National Institutes Using Mobile Phone Data: Estimating Literacy Rates in Senegal, *Journal of the Royal Statistical Society,* Series A, Vol. 180 Issue 4 pp. 1163–1190.

Shim, J., and C. Hwang. 2016. Geographically Weighted Kernel Logistic Regression for Small Area Proportion Estimation. *Journal of the Korean Data and Information Science Society,* 27(2): 531–538.

Sotto, J. C. 2006. *Estimating the Proportion of Underweight Children Aged 0 to 5 Years at the Provincial Level in the Philippines.* Unpublished Special Problem, University of the Philippines, Los Baños.

Sudhakar, K.S. 2009. *Estimation of Number of Households Engaged in Non-farm Activities in Cauvery Command Area Using Small Area Techniques.* Unpublished Thesis, Department of Agricultural Statistics. University of Agricultural Sciences.

Tzavidis, N., Giovanna Rannali, M., Salvati, N., Dreassi, E. and K. Chambers. 2013. Poisson M-quantile Regression for Small Area Estimation. Centre for Statistical and Survey Methodology, University of Wollongong, *Working Paper* 14-13, 28.

Van der Weide, R. 2017. Poverty Mapping at the World Bank. https://psa.gov.ph/content/session-2-1-mr-roy-van-der-weide.

Victoria, J.R.A. 2008. *Estimation of the Unemployment Rates of the Woman and Youth Sectors at the Provincial Level in the Philippines.* Unpublished Master's Thesis, University of the Philippines, Los Baños.

United Nations Department of Economic and Social Affairs (UN DESA). 2000. UN Glossary of Classification Terms: https://unstats.un.org/unsd/classifications/bestpractices/glossary_short.pdf.

United Nations Economic and Social Commission for Asia and the Pacific (UNESCAP). 2019. *Asia and the Pacific SDG Progress Report 2019.* https://www.unescap.org/sites/default/files/Part_III_Data_source_gaps_Asia-Pacific_SDG_Progress_Report2019.pdf.

United Nations Global Pulse. 2012. https://www.unglobalpulse.org/project/measuring-poverty-with-machine-roof-counting/.

Wickham, H. 2013. Tidy Data. *Journal of Statistical Software,* 10(2): 1–24.

World Bank. 2018. Decline of Global Extreme Poverty Continues but Has Slowed: World Bank. https://www.worldbank.org/en/news/press-release/2018/09/19/decline-of-global-extreme-poverty-continues-but-has-slowed-world-bank.

World Health Organization. 1995. Physical Status: The Use and Interpretation of Anthropometry. *WHO Technical Report Series* 854, Geneva, Switzerland.

Yuson, J.M.G. 2012. *Municipal and City Level Estimation of the Total Number of Poor Households in the National Capital and Central Luzon Region in the Philippines.* Unpublished Undergraduate Special Problem, Institute of Statistics. University of the Philippines, Los Baños.

Zhang, X., Onufrak, S., Holt, J.B., and J.B. Croft, J.B. 2013. A Multilevel Approach to Estimating Small Area Childhood Obesity Prevalence at the Census Block-Group Level. *Preventing Chronic Disease.* 10:120252.

www.ingramcontent.com/pod-product-compliance
Lightning Source LLC
Chambersburg PA
CBHW050046220326
41599CB00045B/7307